URBAN PLANNING
IN PRE-COLUMBIAN AMERICA

PLANNING AND CITIES

PLANNING AND CITIES

General Editor

GEORGE R. COLLINS, Columbia University

URBAN PLANNING IN
PRE-COLUMBIAN AMERICA

JORGE HARDOY

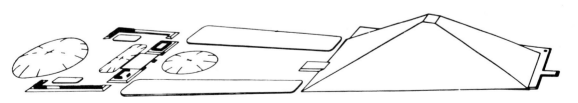

GEORGE BRAZILLER   NEW   YORK

TO MARÍA, INÉS, ISABEL AND AGUSTINA

Copyright © 1968 George Braziller, except in U.S.

For information address the publisher:

George Braziller, Inc.   One Park Avenue   New York, N.Y. 10016

Library of Congress Catalog Card Number: 68–24700

Designed by Jennie Bush

Printed in the Netherlands.

First Printing

CONTENTS

GENERAL EDITOR'S PREFACE

The history of cities, of their physical planning, and of man's theories of urbanism represents a facet of cultural history that is particularly meaningful to us in these years of world-wide urban crisis. Clearly, the dimensions and variety of problems that face us as citizens today are infinitely greater than those of any previous civilization. Nevertheless, it is illuminating for us to examine town structures and ideals of other times and places and to determine how they related to the functioning of the society that was being housed.

It is our hope in this series of books to treat many aspects of urban history and to do so efficiently and in depth by inviting a specialist for each volume who can enlighten us from the vantage point of his own field of competence and his personal enthusiasm for it. We have therefore divided the many titles of our intended survey into a number of categories, such as epochs and areas, theories and models, great planners, and so forth. We have urged our authors to dwell especially on the structural, architectural, and formal components of their subject, not only because these factors seem to be disregarded in the precipitate growth of contemporary cities, but also because the literature on these features of urban history is not at the moment easily accessible to students and interested laymen.

We are commencing with books about epochs and areas. In this historical overview we will range from the root beginnings of the process of urbanism, as seen in settlement patterns of "primitive" man and in the rebirth of towns in Europe during the Middle Ages, to the most sophisticated formulae of baroque despots and of contemporary systems analysts.

G.R.C.

PREFACE

Through the centuries pre-Columbian urbanization shows striking differences from contemporary processes on other continents. Visually, architecturally, and in some ways functionally, Teotihuacán was as different from the Rome of the Caesars as Chan Chan was from Constantinople or Cordova, and Cuzco and Tenochtitlán from Paris, Florence or Genoa. Pre-Columbian cultures tried different principles of urban planning as an answer to the problems posed by sizable and constantly growing cities with complex functional interrelationships, or in order to emphasize and provide an adequate setting for their architectural monuments.

Pre-Columbian urbanization, covering so much territory and hundreds or even thousands of years, is such a vast and complex subject that any analysis would require a much more extensive study than that presented here. The growing interest in the subject shown by scholars of various disciplines suggests that such broader studies will, in time, follow this one. The basic features of those cities where pre-Columbian civilizations synthesized some of their best cultural achievements will then be delineated with greater precision. The aim of the present volume is first of all to survey the process of urbanization in pre-Columbian America, rather than to be inclusive.

Professor George R. Collins of Columbia University, the general editor of the series that includes this book, read a preliminary version of the manuscript and offered valuable suggestions for further organization of the material. With his usual generosity, Dr. Michael Coe of Yale University made available to me his recent studies of the Olmec culture. Last March, in the company of Dr. Carlos Ponce Sanginés, director of the Centro de Investigaciones Tiwanaku, I visited the ruins of that remarkable center in the highlands of Bolivia and benefited from his explanations. To all of these, and to those who through the years have helped me in my research on the urbanization process in Latin America, my sincere thanks.

Jorge Hardoy

Buenos Aires, December 1967

CRITERIA FOR DEFINING A PLANNED CITY IN PRE-COLUMBIAN AMERICA

The subject of this essay is the planned cities of pre-Columbian America—planned cities being those which were presumably created, constructed, or remodeled, at the behest of the power structure, to fulfill certain functions.

Urban planning in pre-Columbian America was a succession of coherent decisions undertaken by highly placed members of the social order who sought to guide or correct the physical development of an urban center. There are few examples of new cities planned from their inception, and none of those achieved great political, religious, or economic influence. The great majority of urban centers grew up spontaneously over the centuries. However, in many cases—especially among the regional capitals—preconceived criteria were imposed to achieve functional clarity, aesthetic effects, or a more rational system of urban circulation.

Pre-Columbian cities performed functions similar to those of almost any city inhabited by a culture in a like stage of development. It is precisely the incorporation and concentration of specific functions on a fixed site that transforms a village into a city or creates a new city. A city is essentially distinguished from a village not only by its greater size and population, more advanced architecture and urban design, and greater social stratification, but by the more complex composition of its labor force and by a way of life that is in every sense more elaborate.

In a previously published study (Hardoy, 1964), I presented criteria for defining pre-Columbian cities of different historical periods and geographical regions whose urbanization preceded the arrival of the Spaniards. Four of these criteria which have particular importance for this volume are: 1) the city had to be a center for the transformation of primary production, including that which might originate outside its immediate zone of influence; 2) it had to be a center of services and, depending on distances, a daily, periodical or occasional market place for the neighboring smaller towns and countryside; 3) it had to fulfill one or more of a series of functions which are specifically urban, such as acting as a political, administrative, religious, cultural or military center, and incorporating the corresponding institutions; and 4) it had to have a high percentage of resident population who also worked there and exhibited a sharp division of labor. None of these cities was self-sufficient, and trade and taxes were undoubtedly as essential in their development as was the concentration of political and religious functions. Planned cities, then, were created or readapted to carry out tasks other than those of merely housing or providing a refuge for their inhabitants.

It is very difficult to distinguish those cities which were deliberately created and planned from those which emerged and grew spontaneously. The data available is limited and there is a scarcity of written, pictorial, or charted information.

Since the end of the pre-Columbian era, numerous planned urban agglomerations have been built wholly or partially, and over-all or partial planning regulations may very well have applied to an entire city. But the creation of a whole new city was an unusual event, and it is unlikely that the majority of pre-Columbian cities were previously planned. In the absence of sources testifying that a city was created, planned, and afterwards developed in accordance with a series of preestablished criteria, it is unacceptable to classify it as "planned" merely because it presents a regular layout.

Many authors have classified as planned all cities which have a regular layout. But in early cultures whose economy was based, for example, on very elementary irrigation, the regular layouts developed naturally as a derivation of the system of land subdivision. Likewise the spontaneous settlement of new territory may have produced population clusters exhibiting a regular layout to meet the need for obtaining an equitable distribution of urban as well as rural lands. In both cases there might have been a consensus of opinion between the participating groups as to the necessity for adopting a regular layout and some form of regulation, instead of allowing the urban area to develop haphazardly. This consensus could have corresponded to ancient forms of organization of a solidary type. The construction of Teotihuacán and Tenochtitlán, the continual reconstructions of Tikal and other Mayan centers, or the remodeling of Cuzco, were planned undertakings; in them the organization of the labor force and its massive deployment went far to make up for the technical limitations of the pre-Columbian cultures.

The socio-political organization which existed in the valley of Teotihuacán during the period of the great constructions was essentially theocratic (Figs. 5–9). It was adapted to the needs of a society more complex and with a greater political and cultural influence beyond the central valley of Mexico than that prevailing there before the appearance of the city.[1] The Pyramid of the Sun and the Pyramid of the Moon are two monumental and totally artificial constructions carried out as a single operation (Figs. 6–7). The builders of the pyramids, of the Citadel, and of the "palacios" of Teotihuacán undertook those constructions without beasts of burden and with no knowledge of iron or the wheel. It is difficult to believe that undertakings of such dimensions and refinement could have been carried out without some centralized administration and without a division of labor that would involve the use of qualified specialists. Some kind of socio-political organization must have existed which could make the decision to plan and design a ceremonial center or to settle on the basic layout of a city and then carry it out.

In pre-Columbian America, urban planning as applied to a sector of a city was not utilized until well-entrenched power groups exercised a total or acceptable measure of control over the political, economic, and social situation. These groups were not necessarily part of a state with an adequate hierarchy for arriving at decisions and with the powers, resources, and organization to implement them. States with strong central control over large territories may have been formed many centuries after the construction of the first planned ceremonial centers, but the societies which constructed such centers were already functioning in accordance with clearly established principles of authority and division of labor. The entrenchment of these power groups within, or independent of, the structure of the state does not necessarily imply that the responsible power group or state would have decided on total or partial planning for the entire area to be occupied by a city, or for a sector of it. But it does mean that a more or less coherent process existed for taking continuous decisions as a consequence of a prolonged and progressive practical experience transmitted from generation to generation within certain cultural contexts. This experience and practice made it possible to adjust certain problems of urban development and foresee others. Societies having the technological level reached by pre-Columbian cultures when the first planned ceremonial centers were constructed would have already possessed the *political and social prerequisites* for decision-making by specified groups and for implementing ambitious rural and urban programs.

In pre-industrial societies, monumentalism as applied to the design of urban agglomerations only appears within certain socio-political contexts. The Egyptians, the Romans during the Empire, the totalitarian monarchs and princes of Europe during the baroque period, all promoted the construction of planned monumental groups of buildings which they incorporated into, or added onto, already existing cities. These cities had not been created or planned, and generally they were already hundreds or even thousands of years old when an individual or a group with sufficient power decided to remodel some sector by putting up a monumental urban complex. In pre-Columbian America something very similar occurred. The large planned ceremonial centers of Teotihuacán (Figs. 5–9), Tiahuanaco (Figs. 38–39) and Tenochtitlán (Figs. 32–37), and the main square of Cuzco (Fig. 55) were constructed on already permanently occupied sites or in the vicinity of them.

It is not easy to determine whether the construction of these four great urban groups, among many others built in the course of centuries by pre-Columbian cultures, was the preponderant factor in the upsurge almost immediately noted in those cities, or if the construction of these groups of buildings was the result of a quickening which was already taking place. The important fact is that the power group with political and social control over the territory where one of those centers was developing decided to incorporate within it a complex of buildings having very precise functions and physical characteristics. *The planning sense of an elite* is shown in such a decision. The technical capacity of the society directed by such an elite, the characteristics of the site, and the material and human resources available in the area within the immediate influence of the place where the complex of buildings was to be constructed had an important influence on its scale, the materials employed, and the design. But the decision was taken with a planning sense endeavoring to put order into the growth of the complex, predetermining the land uses, the functions of the different buildings, and the general criteria of its composition, organizing the urban spaces, the visual sequences and the perspectives in accordance with concepts peculiar to each sub-area and in line with the stage of evolution of the culture occupying it. These are the reasons, perhaps, why Tikal (Figs. 10–13) is so distinct from Teotihuacán of the same period or Cuzco from Chan Chan (Figs. 45–51).

The adoption of standards responsive to the practical necessities of certain societies faced by repeating situations was the principle followed very frequently by pre-Columbian cultures. This signifies that pre-Columbian rulers understood the importance of adopting approved common practices and standards for the solution of similar problems arising from the growth of their urban areas. The builders of Teotihuacán developed a square module which was applied at least to an extensive portion of the central sector. The Aztec rulers, like those of Teotihuacán twelve centuries before, adopted two perpendicular axes, in the center of which they placed key urban functions, which served to regulate the layout of their cities (Tenochtitlán, Fig. 32). The Tiahuanacan expansion into the northern coastal valleys of Peru may be seen in the adoption of a series of interconnected elements forming large enclosures, which seem to have originated in the high central plateau of the Andes, that were systematically applied to the different settlements they constructed. The homogeneity of the solutions is striking. *The repetition of uniform criteria* reveals a functional sense and the importance which the pre-Columbian cultures attached to the utilization of well-tried solutions even though these had not originated within the same culture.

The plan of a city can be just as revealing as artistic styles in an analysis of cultures and their stages of evolution. The disciplined plan of Teotihuacán is unmistakable when compared with the disorderly pattern of settlement which existed around Tikal (Fig. 10). If instead of having them covered by cultivations or destroyed by the jungle we were able to walk through the streets of Teotihuacán or Tikal, the differences observed in the physical plan would be accentuated by those noticed in the type and height of the buildings, the architectural forms, the materials, textures and colors, the use of topography and the relationship between the urban spaces, the symbols and the ornamentation. Lamentably we only have partially complete plans of a very few pre-Columbian cities and for the rest we have nothing but fragmentary information. Moreover, many of the pre-Columbian cities which were inhabited at the time of the conquest were built over by the Spaniards and therefore a complete appreciation of them is now impossible.

The cellular structure is determined by the interrelationship between the spaces and the built-up surfaces, that is to say, essentially between the streets and squares and the blocks of buildings and the isolated constructions. The physical plan of a city is basically the expression of these interrelationships. From a regular urban layout or a cellular urban structure with a high degree of internal homogeneity and formed by the repetition of identical or nearly identical units, it may be anticipated that this was a response to the adoption of clear regulatory criteria which found their expression in the plan. *The regulatory intent reflected in a total or partial urban plan* is, therefore, the only image of an intent to plan which may be discovered today in a pre-Columbian city uninhabited for centuries.

The political and social prerequisites, then, and the planning sense of the governing elite are our determining criteria. They reflect the power of a commanding group in society, its will to make decisions, and its capacity to carry them out. The repetition of uniform criteria and the regulatory intent are the determinative criteria emerging from the first two. Logically, information as to the political and social characteristics of the pre-Columbian cultures can only be verified up to a point. The body of information is, however, continually growing, thus facilitating reconstruc-

12

tion of the organization of the cultures which built the great classical and post-classical cities. And there is also direct knowledge of the cultures which entered into contact with the Spanish conquerors. It is therefore possible to make a tentative analysis of fifteen centuries of pre-Columbian urbanism.

GENERAL CHARACTERISTICS OF URBANIZATION IN PRE-COLUMBIAN AMERICA

Six sub-areas of Middle America* and six sub-areas of South America constitute the geographical basis for an analysis of the pre-Columbian urbanization process (Fig. 1). These are as follows:

IN MIDDLE AMERICA:
Sub-area I: The central coastal region of the Gulf of Mexico extends northwards from the isthmus of Tehuantepec. It has wide forested plains crossed by numerous rivers, swamps, and lagoons. The climate is hot and damp, and the rainfall is among the heaviest in Middle America.

Sub-area II: The central plateau of Mexico has an average altitude of 2,000 meters+ flanked east and west by chains of mountains. Internally it is made up of various valleys separated by high peaks. The climate is temperate owing to the altitude, with dry and moderately cold winters. The geographical situation, in relation to trade potentials, the type of country, the ecological characteristics, and the possibilities for transportation offered by a system of lakes which at one time covered a substantial area created one of the most favorable environments for the life of man and for urban development in pre-Columbian America.

Sub-area III: The high valleys of southern Mexico are few and isolated from one another, favoring the formation of small settlements. In the three long and narrow valleys, fertile and well-watered, in the center of the State of Oaxaca, the Zapotec culture flourished.

Sub-area IV: The highlands of Guatemala have cold and dry winters. It is really a high plateau with high valleys and two large lakes, traversed from north to south by mountain ranges of

*As used here, Middle America comprises Mexico to Honduras.
+1 meter = 39.37 inches.

volcanic origin. Land is cultivated up to a height of 3,000 meters.

Sub-area V: The lowlands of the Petén are covered by thick tropical forests of mahogany, *ceiba, ramon,* fig, *chico zapote,* cedar, and rubber trees which make communications with the other sub-areas difficult. There is an abundance of wild animals and especially birds whose rich plumage was in great demand among pre-Columbian aristocrats. The climate is hot and the heavy rains last from May to January. Limestone is abundant and was used for building purposes. The central zone is a savanna with an average altitude of 150 meters above sea level, crossed by some streams and a series of lakes; but in general, surface water was scarce.

Sub-area VI: The peninsula of Yucatán is an extensive plain without surface waters—dependent on subterranean sources for human consumption and, occasionally, for irrigation. The country is flat, with a slight incline from north to south.

IN SOUTH AMERICA:

Between latitudes 1° and 27° south and between the Andean range and the Pacific coast there is a narrow strip of desert land crossed by numerous intermittently running rivers which flow down from the mountains. Seen from the air the coast is of tremendous formal simplicity, the narrow desert strip alternating with the irrigated green cultivated areas.

Sub-area VII: In the northern coastal region of Peru there are the most extensive and favorable valleys for the development of agriculture with irrigation and of a permanent population. This was true during the pre-Columbian period and it is true now. Of these the most important were the Lambayeque, Jequetepeque, Chicama, and Moche River valleys.

Sub-area VIII: The central coastal region of Peru has characteristics similar to that of the northern coast. The most important valleys were those of the rivers Chancay, Rimac, and Lurin. In size they are intermediate between the valleys of the north and south coasts.

Sub-area IX: In the southern coastal region of Peru the desert is more extensive and the rivers carry less water. The mountains are much nearer the coast. The size of the valleys and their possibilities for settlement were therefore smaller. The most important valleys were those of the rivers Ica and Grande, especially the latter.

Sub-area X: The northern highlands extend from Cajamarca to Chavín de Huantar and up through the Huaraz and Callejón de Huaylas zones. It is formed by a series of longitudinal valleys alternating with mountain ranges. There are great differences in climate according to the height and latitude. Some of the great rivers flowing down from the eastern slopes have their source in this sub-area.

Sub-area XI: The central highlands, like the northern and southern highlands, are formed by a succession of micro-landscapes. The valley of Cuzco lies at its center. The three principal basins, Urubamba, Cuzco, and Anta are situated at an average altitude of over 3,000 meters. The sub-area is intensively cultivated and occupied.

Sub-area XII: The southern highlands have as their center the Puno zone and the Bolivian plateau to the south of Lake Titicaca. It is typycal high-plateau country with altitudes near to or above 3,900 meters. The climate and soil of the *puna* make certain cultivations difficult, but it is ideal for the rearing of llamas and alpacas.

Every one of these twelve sub-areas was an important center of civilization during the centuries which witnessed the development of pre-Columbian urban cultures. Not all of them reached similar peaks, nor did they arrive at them simultaneously. During some stage of their development, one or more of these sub-areas acted as a nuclear area with respect to the rest, that is to say, as "an area of concentrated economic and demographic power" in which a more advanced form of urbanism took place.[2] This appears to have been the role of sub-area I during the formative period or of sub-area II during the classic period in Middle America and of sub-area XI in South America during the expansion of the Inca culture. But also the participation and gravitation of some of the sub-areas in the cultural development of Middle America, such as sub-area V, ceased at the close of the classic period for reasons not very well explained. In general, at different periods, certain sub-areas assumed dependent roles as a consequence of inverse relationship between the dynamism of some, and the stagnation, disintegration, and change in the structures of others. On more than one occasion expansions must have occurred with military backing, which characterized, under a more or less centralized system of government, various of the sub-areas of Middle or of South America. For instance, during the century immediately preceding the Spanish conquest, and coinciding with the militarist period, the six sub-areas of South America remained under a single central control whose influence was felt even farther to the north and south. This was also true of sub-areas I, II, and III in Middle America at the same time.

In these twelve sub-areas, which comprise no more than five per cent of the territory of today's Latin America, a very high percentage of the total pre-Columbian population was concentrated. Nearly all of the sub-areas were permanently occupied during various millennia, from the pre-ceramic centuries until the Spanish conquest. But not all of the twelve sub-areas are of similar interest, nor did urbanization take place in all of them with equal intensity. In some, geographical and ecological conditions favored the formation of better interconnected urban systems and more extensive cities. The size, climate and soil of the immediate environment and its location with reference to other sub-areas with different types of production were in this respect of fundamental importance.

The process of urbanization in pre-Columbian Middle and South America proceeded more or less simultaneously (Fig. 2). No doubt an interchange of ideas between both areas existed from the formative stages and was possibly intensified during the classic and post-classic periods. The bases therefore existed for the stages and characteristics of both urbanization processes to be relatively similar and simultaneous. Nevertheless, an analysis of the results of these processes clearly shows that the classic and post-classic cities of Middle America were urbanistically more complete and architecturally more monumental and refined than those of South America.

Finally, it should be pointed out that urbanization in Middle America and South America did not grow steadily with the passing of time. On the contrary, they were step-by-step processes having different moments of culmination. In Middle America there were at least two periods of upsurge interrupted by an acute decline in urban life (Figs. 2–3). The first of these periods is represented by the flourishing of the classic cities. Between the second and seventh centuries A.D., Teotihuacán flourished in the center of Mexico (Figs. 5–9), and between the third and ninth centuries A.D. the Mayan centers of the Usumacinta River valley, such as Palenque (Figs. 14–15), Yaxchilán (Fig. 16) and Piedras Negras (Figs. 17–18), and of the Petén, like Tikal (Figs. 10–13) and Uaxactún (Fig. 20). Other centers reached their highest peak some time afterwards, although they took part in the general rebirth of the classic cultures of Middle America: El Tajín (Figs. 27–28) on the coast of the Gulf of Mexico, Xochicalco (Figs. 25–26) at the western end of the valley of Mexico, Monte Albán on the highlands of Oaxaca (Figs. 29–30), and Dzibilchaltún, Cobá, Oxkintok, and other centers in Yucatán.

Later, there was an interlude of centuries during which a decline took place in almost all the sub-areas. In the Petén, a way of life which we could classify for that time and place as urban disappeared altogether. The causes of this decline are not precisely known; there is no doubt, however, that invasions from the north by tribes with a lower cultural level than the classic cultures, but with superior vitality and martial spirit, had a lot to do with it. Between the 10th and 12th centuries, Tula, the Toltec capital, was the principal city of the central plateau of Mexico and the inheritor of the culture, the art, and the power which, centuries before, Teotihuacán had possessed. However, Tula never attained the brilliance or influence of Teotihuacán. It was burned by invaders from the north about 1224 and abandoned for good some fifty years after. In this way a new but not as marked decline took place in urban life in central Mexico.

The second upsurge commenced in the 14th century and continued until the conquest of Mexico by the Spaniards. In the cities of central Mexico, in Tenochtitlán, Texcoco, Tlacopán, Azcapotzalco, Cholula, Ixtapalapa, and others, urban life was highly developed and commerce took place on a scale which had never before existed in any region of Middle America. From the importance of their institutions, from the number and variety of specialists dedicated to the production of goods for local consumption and for export to other regions, and from the almost total dependence on imported food products to sustain the urban population which, to a high degree, was dedicated to activities other than the primary industries, it may be concluded that in the centuries immediately preceding the Spanish conquest, the cities of central Mexico may have represented the culmination of the urbanization process in Middle America.

Urban life had a second rebirth in the sub-areas which were under the military influence of the Aztec confederation and paid tribute to it. Mitla, in the high valleys of Oaxaca, and Cempoala, on the coast of the Gulf of Mexico, became pre-eminent in their respective sub-areas, whereas the Mayan cities of Yucatán, of which Chichén-Itzá may be taken as typical, after a period of rise which continued until the 13th century, entered into a prolonged period of decline up to the time of the Spanish conquest of the peninsula commencing in 1527.

In the history of the pre-Columbian cultures in the six sub-areas of South America there were three points at which the relative independence of their development was interrupted by religious or religious-cum-military movements which introduced a high degree of stylistic homogeneity into several of the sub-areas. The first point was represented by Chavín, towards the middle of the second millennium B.C., when the cultures of the coast and of the highlands were still a long way from reaching the urban stage. In the central Andes, in the second and perhaps the third millennium B.C., permanent communities surrounding ceremonial centers were constructed along lines which anticipated future developments in the central plateau and on the east coast of Mexico.[3]

The second point was that of the expansion of the Tiahuana-can culture which commenced in the second half of the first millennium A.D. Undoubtedly this was supported by military groups and was carried on for centuries of intense military activity. The introduction of the Tiahuanacan style on the coast terminated the classic styles, notably that of the Mochica on the northern coast and of the Nazca on the south. This Tiahuanacan expansion also marked the commencement of the urbanistic period on the coast. For the first time real cities were built, re-placing the large villages of the classic cultures.

The third point was represented by the Incas. Their area of influence was the most extensive, covering all six sub-areas (Fig. 61), but it was only of brief duration and did not manage to last a century. It was a period of great military and construction activity, when large programs of regional infrastructure were undertaken. But urbanistically it was not a period of innovation like the Tiahuanacan. All three movements arose in the high-lands. The prosperous coastal cultures, developing in a more propitious environment, seem to have been the target of these expansionist movements.

The urbanization process on the coast appears to have fol-lowed a continuous upward trend which, in the northern and central coastal valleys, reached its peak during the centuries intervening between the Tiahuanacan and Inca expansions. During those centuries, when the Chimú empire was consoli-dated, Chan Chan, its capital and perhaps the most extensive city of pre-Columbian Peru, was constructed. On the other hand, the urbanization process in the highlands underwent more pronounced ups and downs. Huari, possibly the hub of Tiahua-nacan culture, and Cuzco, the Inca capital, represent the peak periods of urbanization in the highlands.

THE GOLDEN AGE OF URBANIZATION IN CENTRAL MEXICO

Nearly all published chronologies of the cultural development of Middle and South America during the pre-Columbian period commence with the epoch of the hunters and farmers. The origins are unprecise but it may be assumed that about 8,000 years ago a large part of the continental territory, and especially the more favorable of the sub-areas, had already been penetrated for more or less prolonged periods, inhabited by groups of hunters and food-gatherers.[4]

Agriculture and pottery were as yet unknown. The groups of nomadic hunters followed natural routes determined by the topography, pausing to sojourn according to the possibilities of the local environment. At some time or other they had to arrive at more perfected and permanent forms of subsistence which allowed them to adapt themselves to different ecological conditions. In the central plateau of Mexico, for example, changes in climate produced a dispersion of the fauna and extinction of the large mammals which were the principal source of food for the hunters. But the technological innovations dating from that time showed that the hunters were capable of exploiting their environment and of advancing to new stages in their cultural development.

Between 6000 and 2000 B.C. in the center of Mexico, and between 4000 and 800 B.C. in the river valleys of the Peruvian coast, the population became more dense. Parallel with this, agricultural techniques were perfected and the manufacture of the necessary implements for sowing, harvesting and storage began, while plants suitable for human consumption were cultivated and the first permanent villages were constructed. Maize, a variety of beans and squashes, peanuts, and chili peppers were already staples among the early farming communities of Middle and South America; the potato and the quinoa were cultivated in the Andean highlands; cotton textiles were known by all pre-Columbian urban cultures. Milling stones, baskets, and pottery were fully developed, contributing toward a permanent, settled community life.

At the beginning of the second millennium B.C. agricultural communities with a sufficient variety of resources were present in almost all of the sub-areas mentioned. Hunting and food-gathering in all the sub-areas, and fishing off the sea coast of Peru and in the lake districts, made important contributions to the diet, but agriculture and horticulture had developed sufficiently to constitute the main source of sustenance. With a better diet and a growing food supply the inhabitants of the small self-sufficient villages gradually advanced toward a way of life which was progressively urban, as reflected in the larger scale of the agglomerations, in the construction of the first religious buildings, and in the gradual specialization of labor.

Between 1200 and 400 B.C. a pattern of small compact villages or of a denser rural population concentrated around a temple-pyramid nucleus was frequently encountered. This pattern is generally accepted as reflecting the importance attained by the priestly class, whose power was based on a growing prestige; it prefaces the urbanistic period in all the sub-areas. It is represented possibly by Tlatilco and more surely by Cuicuilco in central Mexico, by San Lorenzo and later by La Venta (Fig. 4) on the Gulf coast, by Monte Albán (Fig. 29–30) in Oaxaca, by Chiapa del Corzo in Chiapas, by Kaminaljuyú in the highlands of Guatemala, by Uaxactún (Fig. 20), Tikal (Figs. 10–13), Seibal, and Altar de Sacrificios in the Petén, and by a similar model in Yucatán, possibly on the very site of Dzibilchaltún; by Chavín de Huantar and Kotosh in the Peruvian highlands, and by the mounds found on the northern coast of Peru. There is no doubt that it was a pattern repeated with regional differences throughout the sub-areas of Middle and South America and that it responded to increasing social differentiations and technological development.

Whether the priestly class commenced to function as a political group, bringing together various villages under centralized control, or remained in a secondary role, leaving the affairs of state in the hands of hereditary families with control over certain territories, is still subject to discussion. The relevant fact is the growth of an elite with total or almost total control over the decision-making processes reflected in the theocratic character which the pre-Columbian societies gradually acquired. At the beginning of the first millennium B.C., and perhaps still earlier, there was an evident consolidation of parallel systems of authoritarian socio-political organization, with considerable power concentrated in the hands of a small elite exclusively occupied with the task of government, of regulating the religious cults, and developing the styles symbolizing them. The establishment of this class and the consolidation of a new socio-political order are reflected in the construction of ceremonial centers having a scale and a complexity of design hitherto unknown.

Toward the end of the second millenium and the beginning of the first millenium B.C. the Olmec culture developed on the coast of the Gulf of Mexico.[5] In the principal centers of this culture, Tenochtitlán, Laguna de los Cerros, Tres Zapotes, and hundreds of minor centers, but especially in San Lorenzo and La Venta (Fig. 4), monumental sculpture in stone reached one of the climaxes of pre-Columbian realistic art. Although there is some question as to whether the Olmec culture was of tropical origin or descended from the highlands of Morelos, Puebla, or Guerrero to the coast, it is generally accepted that it had decisive bearing on the formation of the classic cultures of Middle America. Covarrubias has called it the Mother Culture, others regard it as the most ancient of the high cultures of Middle America. For the present, we accept the earliest known Olmec occupation of San Lorenzo, and its monuments, as belonging to the early formative period, and place the heyday of La Venta between 800 and 400 B.C., in other words, centuries before the emergence of the urban civilization of Teotihuacán and other Middle American cultures, such as the Zapotec and the Maya in Yucatán, in the Petén and in the highlands of Guatemala.

If various aspects of Olmec influence are evident in the development of the high cultures of Middle America it may well be asked if this was also the case with urbanization. At the time when Olmec social organization and engineering was in full flower, one of the first ceremonial centers on a monumental scale and of totally original conception was planned and built in La Venta (Fig. 4). Its ceremonial complex was constructed around 800 B.C. and destroyed and abandoned four centuries later.[6] The site selected by the builders was a long, dry and irregularly shaped island of some 500 to 600 hectares* surrounded by swamps, in the bed of the river Tonalá. The site is isolated and ill-suited to the construction of houses; the builders of La Venta, like those of San Lorenzo and other Olmec centers, had to carry the basalt for the monuments from sources far from the site. Moreover, the ecological characteristics of the territory surrounding La Venta and San Lorenzo could not support a large population.

Some sense of the socio-political organization and planning ability of the governing elite is conveyed by the choice of a site which, lacking the necessary conditions for a permanent agglomeration and for a strategic commercial location, necessitated the coordination of numerous groups of workmen brought seasonally from distant places to get out the stone, prepare it, transport it, and finally convert it into architecture and sculpture. Considering the low technological level of the Olmecs, an enterprise of such a scale must have drained a large amount of labor from agriculture and productive tasks in general. This labor may have been secured up to a point through religious fervor, but it was more probably the result of some form of coercion obtainable only in a clearly stratified authoritarian society. The size of the projects and the organizing ability required to carry them on clearly reveal a centralized control of decision making. La Venta was not a city. It did not have a numerous permanent population residing within it; possibly the only inhabitants were the attendants of the temple. Few burials have been discovered. Large crowds may have gathered occasionally for ceremonies at the site, but the periodic rituals would have been carried out in complete isolation. The power of the elite did not necessitate their living together with the agricultural workers; their prestige

*1 hectare = 2.47 acres.

21

and control must have been obtained and exercised in some other way.

The orientation of the ceremonial center of La Venta, at 8° west of north, has the north-south alignment characteristic of Olmec ceremonial centers at that time, such as San Lorenzo and Laguna de los Cerros, as well as other classic complexes of Middle America. The group is composed from south to north by three principal elements: a pyramid with a rectangular base of 140 by 80 meters and a maximum height of nearly 35 meters oriented in the same general direction as the group; a transitional space flanked laterally by two low pyramidal platforms with rectangular bases; and lastly, a ceremonial square set at right angles to the orientation of the group and surrounded by basalt columns mounted on a low wall.

The feeling of the Olmec builders for symmetry was evident. The plateau where San Lorenzo was built was artificially remodeled to achieve a symmetrical shape for the whole 25-hectare surface. Logically, the location of the monuments and sculptures also tended to follow symmetrical arrangements.[7]

The ceremonial center of La Venta was organized symmetrically along a principal axis, but certain minor details were introduced, such as the placement of certain altars or stelae, which deviate from this axial criterion. A single axis leads from the colonnaded square to the intermediate open area and thence to the temple's access stairway, constituting an intentional sequence of two spaces by way of a progression toward the pyramid. This may well have been the first time a sequence of this kind was projected in Middle America. It may also have been in the Olmec area that the combination of a sloping embankment or batter *(talud)* with a vertical rectangular panel *(tablero)* was used for the first time in the walls of pyramidal constructions, a combination which was afterwards to be repeated in classic and postclassic buildings in central Mexico and other sub-areas of Middle America.

There is a gap of four or more centuries between the abandonment of La Venta and the rise of Teotihuacán as a city. Although we do not have a general picture of the principal events of those centuries, we may assume that the population grew and densified under relatively peaceful conditions, as revealed by the styles of art. We may also assume that increased concentration of the population led to formation of the preconditions on which urban life were based in that period and region.

From the very last centuries of the first millennium B.C., Teotihuacán was the residence of a large and permanent population occupied in government duties, services, trade, and handicrafts without the necessity to leave the city to earn their living. This

22

situation constituted a fundamental change in the organization of labor from that of the agricultural villages of the formative period, when all able-bodied men and—seasonally—even the women and children left their homes to go into the fields, or as compared to a purely ceremonial center like La Venta. The urban structure and layout of Teotihuacán must, therefore, have been prepared to deal with all of the characteristic functions of a true city. What we know of its plan reflects the various hierarchies that these functions assumed with respect to the activities already incorporated into the urban life of the classic cultures in the central plateau of Mexico.

The valley of Teotihuacán was occupied during the formative period by a rural population living in small settlements located along the slopes of the valley (Sanders, 1965). The process of densification and nucleation was slow through the formative period and was characterized by a gradual migration of the settlements toward the alluvial plain. Between 100 B.C. and 100 A.D. an urban center nucleated half or more of the population of the valley in one permanent settlement, possibly as a consequence of increased social differentiations and changes in the use of land. The city was built in a flat sector in the central section of the valley having a gentle slope from north to south.

The valley of Teotihuacán is a branch of the central valley of Mexico with an altitude of 2,200 meters above sea level. The valley has a total surface of around 25,000 hectares and is flanked by two parallel ranges of mountains having a height of some 600 meters above that of the archaeological zone. Only half of the valley's land is suitable for cultivation, although it may have been centuries of deforestation and erosion that reduced the valley's potentials. The principal topographical feature is the narrow San Juan River which runs from east to west parallel with the mountains. There are few minor elevations in the valley, but none in the section selected for the construction of the city.

The ceremonial center of Teotihuacán (Figs. 5–6) was started and finished in the course of the first three or four centuries of the Christian Era. Later it was modified in appearance with the incorporation of certain religious groups of secondary importance and "palaces" which bordered the principal central axis of movement, but layout, scale, and general characteristics were respected. The Citadel was built about the third or fourth century A.D., its architecture more refined and detailed than that of the two pyramids belonging to a previous period. A large enclosure was discovered a few years ago in front of the Citadel, also organized around a sunken central square. The functions of this square are not very clear, but it may have been the commercial center of the city (Millon, 1967).

23

The system of circulation in the city was the most simple and functional solution that could be found. The city was constructed around a cruciform scheme, and nothing existed or has appeared which would have justified any different pattern.

At the crossing of the two principal axes stood the Citadel and the large enclosure which is said to have been given over to commercial activities. The direction of the streets of the city was controlled by the orientation of these two axes (Fig. 5). The north-south axis has a deviation of 15.5° east of north. It acted as a linear core and it is now called Calle de los Muertos (Street of the Dead). It was the great processional avenue and movement artery of the city center. The principal religious monuments of the city are connected with one another by means of this street. The Street of the Dead extends from the Pyramid of the Moon at the north to far southward beyond the Citadel (Fig. 6). Its length was more than 6,000 meters. By means of several groups of stairs and a gentle slope, the builders were able to overcome a difference in level through the whole of this distance which, from the extreme north to the Citadel, viz., in less than half the total distance, was already 30 meters. The east-west axis extends at right angles to the Street of the Dead for a distance of more than 3,000 meters on either side. As it has only recently been discovered, its architectural and engineering characteristics have not yet been properly established.

The monumentalism of the Street of the Dead was unique in pre-Columbian America and its axial perspective is a subtle example of the progression which can be obtained by simple but well-related means (Fig. 7). The street had a width of 45 meters and was visually urban in every sense, surrounded as it was by a succession of "palaces" and temples and somewhat sunken compared with the level of the bases upon which these constructions rested (Fig. 8). For the walker who started from the point of union of the two axes, in front of the principal access to the Citadel (Fig. 9), the climax was the Pyramid of the Moon, more than two kilometers* away. A good part of the difference in level was made up by the time he had gone half the way. By the simple expedient of grouping stairs, the builders had obliged him to interrupt the rhythm of his walk at least five times and so distract his attention momentarily from his destination. Along the whole first half of his route, the Pyramid of the Sun, greatest of all the pyramids of Teotihuacán, could be seen in continually changing perspective according to the rhythm he adopted.[8] The slope of the embankments in the top part makes it appear lower and very much heavier, but its proportions are equally majestic

*1 kilometer = .62 miles

24

and its presence dominates the whole of this sector of the Street of the Dead.[9]

The eccentric position of the Pyramid of the Sun, without a corresponding mass to balance a volume which in itself is deliberately symmetrical and bilateral, has always surprised me. It is also somewhat inexplicable that in such a formal urban organization there was no avenue facing the principal and western facade of the Pyramid of the Sun, which might perhaps have given it a perspective vista consonant with the monumentalism that governs the general composition. Having passed the Pyramid of the Sun, entry is made into the final sector of the Street of the Dead before arriving, five hundred meters further ahead, at a square plaza 130 meters wide and surrounded by the classic staired pyramids with their regular bases and flat tops. This square acts as an atrium or open antechamber before reaching the Pyramid of the Moon and the four flights of stairway that serve as its access. The sobriety of the religious architecture of Teotihuacán is enhanced by the simple urbanistic disposition already described. Its urban spaces have their limits precisely set by the masses; there are no colonnades or other semi-open urban spaces. Everything was accomplished with the minimum number of elements: architecturally, by employing truncated pyramidal masses composed of a series of sloped embankments *(taludes)*, alternating, in the smaller constructions, with vertical panels *(tableros);* and urbanistically, by making use of the simplest of signs utilized from the remotest times when possession was taken of a place, namely two axes crossing one another at right angles. This was not the first time that such a sign was utilized in the history of urbanism but it certainly was for America.

THE MAYAS

The urban conception of the Mayas was totally distinct from that prevailing during the same period in central Mexico. In every Mayan settlement a clear differentiation has to be made between 1) the central complex, organized around a group of plazas, courtyards and platforms surrounded by stepped pyramids, "palaces" and other constructions fulfilling ceremonial and possibly residential functions, 2) an intermediate sector, and 3) the agricultural countryside. Because of their higher concentration of buildings and superior architecture the central complex and the intermediate sector may be qualified as urban by comparison with the countryside, although they had neither the density nor the layout nor the visual characteristics of what would be considered as urban today, or even then, among other Middle American cultures. Nevertheless, these three sectors, namely the agricultural, the intermediate, and the central, would be clearly distinguished by anyone approaching a Mayan center.

First came the jungle and the *milpas* or farms, then the clusters of houses built over low platforms, possibly surrounded by some small cultivated plots and, lastly, one or more monumental centers formed by ceremonial buildings and "palaces." Apparently there were no causeways or roads expressly delineated for connecting the Mayan centers. The pedestrian traveled along pathways marked out in the course of time by the accidents of the terrain. The discovery of an isolated causeway linking two major centers does not justify the supposition that there existed a network of properly constructed and permanently maintained roads, even within a limited area.[10]

A greater part of Mayan territory was occupied by the *milpas*, whose frequency increased with their proximity to a center inhabited permanently by groups not directly occupied in primary production. Density in the agricultural area was very low. If we assume that an economic unit during the first millennium A.D. in the zone of Tikal was similar to one today in the San José area on the banks of Lake Petén-Itzá, each family nucleus of five persons required about two hectares.[11] This means a density of two and a half persons per hectare, if the territory had been evenly occupied, but it looks as if distribution could not have been even because of differences in the quality of land. To begin with, it is unlikely that the *milpero* would have lived isolated in a dwelling erected on his farm. It is more likely that the great majority lived together just as they do at present, in small unplanned hamlets or in groups of two, three, or four houses—placed with the supply of water and the height of the land in mind—from which they would go off to their *milpas* either every day, or for stays of a week or longer according to the distances to be covered and the needs of their crops.

The vicinity of a center would have been indicated by an increasing density of population. The *milpa* country, interspersed with jungle, gradually gave way to a countryside more densely dotted with groups of two, three, and even four thatched wooden structures on square platforms among the trees, observing no order other than that of avoiding the *bajos*—those low-lying patches in danger of the inundation so common in the Petén.

The plan of Tikal shows the urban structure of a Mayan center in the Petén at the end of the classic period (Fig. 10) and that of Mayapán, a post-classic center in Yucatán (Fig. 19). In both of them, the water sources—the wells or *cenotes* in Yucatán and the reservoirs and lagoons in Tikal—were a partial densifying factor. Neither shows any system of streets, and movement evidently took place along trails or pathways; a preference is seen for more elevated building sites.

Here and there, among the houses, the trees, and the low-lying parts of this intermediate sector, the temples or groups of temples and "palaces" were constructed. In Tikal, the Temple of the Inscriptions, the north zone group, and Temple IV are united to the central square by broad causeways. There is no order to be seen in the distribution of the groups or the single temples over the mapped area of 16 square kilometers. In all cases high zones, but not necessarily the highest, were the preferred building sites. This factor of location, and the fact that access to these isolated temples and clusters of buildings was gained by causeways, may indicate the existence of a predetermined sense of hierarchical order and an urbanistic interest in adequate connections between groups of buildings which, we can assume, had similar or complementary functions.

The complex of temples, "palaces," squares, courtyards, and platforms constructed around the Great Square was the true center of Tikal. The three principal causeways converged upon it. Only one smaller group, the southwest group, stood alone, disconnected from the main movement system to be found in Tikal. The width of the causeways was no doubt excessive for the day-to-day movement of the populace. Possibly they were intended for processions or other ceremonial activities.[12] In the remainder of the mapped area—in which the stable population may have reached something above 10,000 inhabitants, although a great many more from the surrounding country must have passed through it daily on their way to and from the central complex—no signs of streets or roads have been found.

There is something very special about the urban structure of Tikal, brought about exclusively by topographical considerations. The biggest surprise is that Tikal had no clear access. Even though there was no road network linking Tikal with the nearest centers in the *bajo* country of northeastern Petén, such as Uaxactún, Yaxhá, Nakum, El Encanto, Chunhuitz, Naranjo, Holmul, Tikinchakán, Xunantunich and others, it might have been expected that some trail or other, when nearing any of these centers, would have been transformed into a causeway leading to the central complex. There is no evidence, however, that this occurred. Tikal has a centripetal structure whose central group acts as a pivot for the other three nuclei, completely disconnected from the nearby dwelling sector and the surrounding environment.

The central complex grew from century to century and was constantly enlarged and perfected up to the time of its gradual abandonment. All the architectural styles of Tikal adopted in the course of more than a millennium are represented there, frequently superimposed one upon the other. Like all the great urban complexes of the world, the central group of Tikal grew but slowly. Its history goes back to perhaps 600 B.C., when the first groups of people established themselves there.[13] The North Acropolis was one of the selected sites, as discoveries of ceramics show. The oldest architecture known, dating from the third and second centuries B.C., consisted of simple masonry platforms constructed with yellow stone of the locality. The preferred site was the highest around, there being natural drainage, and its position was dramatized by declivities to the north and east. It was here that, with the passage of time, the astounding complex of temples and platforms known as the North Acropolis was to emerge. It is quite certain that this was never conceived, any more than was the Great Square, as a unique and definitive work.

The central group of Tikal is one of the most original complexes in urban history (Fig. 11). All the great elements of urban design are concentrated there in a partially occupied area of 75 hectares. The Great Square is the climax, where the most significant religious and civil functions of Tikal were carried out (Fig. 13). The approach to it was provided by three causeways which allowed changing perspectives of the most important buildings of Tikal; their breadth contrasts with the sense of spatial confinement invoked by the spectacular group of constructions that formed the city's framework. Vertical force was provided by the two temples facing one another and constructed almost simultaneously about 700 A.D. (Fig. 12). Of all the large constructions of Tikal these two temples, resting on the elevated platforms,[14] are perhaps the best proportioned, their airiness enhanced by elaborate painted crests. Although Temples I and II face each other and at first sight give the impression that their single stairways are aligned along the same east-west axis, a slight deviation exists nevertheless.

Temples I and II close off the square on the east and west. The embankment upon which the Central Acropolis was constructed sets a clear-cut massive limit to the south that contrasts with the more fluid group of temples and their stairways which form the North Acropolis. The North Acropolis rests on a wide platform descending in the form of a broad and gradual stairway down to the level of the square. There is no doubt that the North Acropolis or the site upon which it was placed had some special significance for the Mayas. In no other place in Tikal was such intense and continuous reconstruction carried on over such a long period of time—a thousand years.[15]

The Central Acropolis was of a totally different conception; it probably fulfilled residential, storage, and general civic functions, and not specifically religious ones. The high pyramids are absent; in their stead, there are numerous buildings of the "palace" type, whose function still intrigues investigators. The impression given by the Central Acropolis is one of mass and extraordinary architectural force. The constructions in stone are organized around several courtyards of varying shape and size with some meters of difference in level between them. There are no axes of composition, not even in the organization of a single square. The two hectares occupied by the Central Acropolis give the impression of having been constructed without any prior planning, although the group may have been completed within a short period. Architecturally, the "palaces" are of little interest. For the Mayas, architectural space was of no particular significance. Technically limited to small spans which rarely exceed two or two and a half meters, their buildings have damp, dark interiors and long narrow ground plans.

But in their treatment of urban spaces, the Mayas did reach one of the peaks we know of in the history of urban design. The ceremonial centers of Tikal, of Copán, Palenque (Figs. 14–15), Piedras Negras (Figs. 17–18), Yaxchilán (Fig. 16), or Uaxactún (Fig. 20) were true works of art. Despite the destruction of some of them it is nevertheless still possible to appreciate the skill in taking advantage of topography, the incredible subtlety displayed in the modelling of sequences, the deliberate handling of the element of surprise, and a clear intention to avoid monumental axes. Although limited in technique, working with only a few architectural forms and urban elements such as the pyramid, the platform, the low wall or embankment, stairways of varied size and gradient, and stelae, they arrived at the desired aesthetic unity. The beauty of the Mayan ceremonial centers resides in the extraordinary variety of formal combination they present, from various vantage points, to the visitor.

These magnificent displays of artistic sensibility cannot have been merely improvised. Those who visit the Maya centers will not, of course, find the axial monumentality or the extended perspective of the linear progression of Teotihuacán. As in the great medieval complexes of Italy, there was a slow evolution in Tikal, completed stage by stage and perfected until, at the closing of the late classic period, just before the abandonment of the city, it attained the form we now know.[16]

All the Maya centers present notable differences in organization. The most perfected examples of the exploitation of topography to obtain aesthetic effects are the classic centers of the Usumacinta valley. In Yaxchilán, Piedras Negras, and Palenque, in the seventh and eighth centuries A.D., the sculptural art of the Mayas reached its greatest splendor. The centers of Yaxchilán and Piedras Negras were constructed on top of cliffs bordering the Usumacinta River which, during the classic centuries, was one of the principal communication routes connecting the Petén and the interior with the coastal sites on the Gulf of Mexico.

Notably in Yaxchilán, the top of the cliff was leveled off and landscaped to provide space for some fifty constructions which extend about 600 meters parallel to the river (Fig. 16). Moving along this platform from southeast to northwest, one crosses several big squares to reach—by means of a wide intermediate space—the great square which is closed off at its northeast end by a pyramidal type of construction set on a wide platform. This was no doubt the most important building in Yaxchilán.

The controlled vistas toward the river or toward the broken country, with their groups of constructions at the top of the most prominent mounds, were no doubt intentional. As in Tikal, there is no axial composition evident in Yaxchilán. The complex is treated as if it were an open-air museum of sculpture. There are no colonnades or semitransparent architectural elements of transition. There is only the simple handling of the masses in relation to one another and to the landscape.

The same criteria appear in Piedras Negras, but they are more dramatically emphasized by the fifty-meter difference in level between the eastern or principal square, and the river, and the location of the acropolis at a height of 80 meters above the river and 30 meters above the square (Fig. 18). A sequence of steeply graded stairways followed by courtyards gives access to the central quadrangle of slightly trapezoidal shape, bordered by classic buildings having a long and narrow ground plan (Fig. 17). In Piedras Negras, as in other Maya centers, the squares are irregular as the result of the location of the constructions, for which the most elevated sites were selected.

The Toltec or Mexican influence is very important in the cultural life of the Mayas of Yucatán after the collapse of the classic civilizations around the ninth and tenth centuries. These foreign groups, exiled from their homeland in central Mexico, forced upon the Maya the cult of Quetzalcoatl, the feathered serpent god, and introduced substantial changes in the local sculpture, architecture and urban design.

Chichén-Itzá was the new capital of the invaders and remained the key religious center of Yucatán for more than two centuries.[17] A new people of Chontal-Maya origin, the Itzá, became the main force in Yucatán and founded Mayapán as their capital sometime during the 13th century. The decline of Mayapán left the peninsula in a state of anarchy which persisted until the arrival of the

Spanish conquerors when the 16th century was already well advanced. What Montejo and his men saw had few reminiscences of the classic splendor achieved at Uxmal, Chichén-Itzá, Cobá, Dzibilchaltún, Kayal, Etzna and other centers.[18]

Tulum is unique in Maya urbanism (Fig. 21). Solitary on the east coast of Yucatán, its origin may date from the classic period, possibly the sixth century A.D., and although its form and definitive layout are, of all the Maya centers, those most nearly approaching our idea of a city, they must have acquired their final characteristics centuries later during the post-classic period, coincidentally with the emergence of Mayapán as a regional capital (Fig. 21). Tulum presents two characteristics which are unexampled among the Mayas. First, the ground plan, a rectangle of 380 by 170 meters, is surrounded on three sides—the fourth is a precipice over the sea—by a wall of up to five meters in width and an average height of between three and five meters (Fig. 22). Second, and in relation to the gateways in the walls, parallel urban streets appear, flanked in a visually continuous manner by different constructions. I am not aware that any antecedents exist in any of the other Maya centers for this, nor that it has been repeated elsewhere. The Mexican influence to be noted in the architecture of The Castle (El Castillo), the principal building of Tulum, may have had some bearing on the original layout of the city.

POST-CLASSIC URBANIZATION
IN MIDDLE AMERICA

The abandonment of Teotihuacán brought a decline of urban life in central Mexico which lasted some three hundred years. It was a period of political disintegration and cultural stagnation which came to an end when a group new to the area took control of the situation and restored administrative unity and urban conditions. The Toltecs, like most of the invaders of central Mexico, came from the north. At the end of the tenth century they founded a city about 80 kilometers northwest of Teotihuacán which is known by the name of Tula and was their capital and the cult center of the god Quetzalcoatl.

Tula was founded by Ce Acatl Topiltzin, the son of a famous war lord who led the Toltecs in their invasion of central Mexico.[19] In a few years the influence of the Toltecs and the artistic renaissance generated in their capital was felt all over Middle America. In due time Toltec architecture and styles of art were transferred to Yucatán, after Mexican groups had taken political control of the area and made Chichén-Itzá their cultural center. Tula grew to a considerable size, despite its having been plundered and burned only two hundred and fifty years after it was founded. It introduced certain innovations in urban design and architecture. Toltec architecture is one of the best attempts at artistic integration to be found among pre-Columbian cultures, with a masterly combination of strong colors and realistic representations of animals, warriors and abstract forms (Fig. 23).

Nothing is known of the over-all layout of the city. The ruins of "palaces," following the traditional courtyard model of central Mexico, have been found spread over a large surface. The design of the main square reveals a transition between the monumental linear center of Teotihuacán and the clustered type favored by the Aztecs. The main square of Tula was an open space of some 120 meters on each side, closed to the north by a colonnaded hall built on a platform which also supported the pyramid of Quetzalcoatl and several buildings of the "palace" type, and to the east by a stepped pyramid with a stairway facing the square (Fig. 24). In contrast, the west and south sides of the square left vistas open. In other words, it was not an enclosed and symmetrical space with one main access, like the one fronting the Pyramid of the Moon at Teotihuacán; it was an attempt to find a more flexible solution to the visual continuity beyond the limits of the square, based on the already known principle of combining and balancing free-standing forms.

Three other cities are worthy of mention—Xochicalco, El Tajín and Monte Albán, geographically located at intermediate areas between the dominant centers of central Mexican and Mayan culture.

It is possible that the apogee of Xochicalco (Fig. 25) came after the decline of Teotihuacán. There are many evidences of a stylistic link between Tula and this large city located on the western slopes of central Mexico, just as there are relations between Xochicalco's architectural forms, functions, and ornamentation and those of the Mayas. Undoubtedly the superb and detailed use of topography at Xochicalco was quite different from the more rational and functional approach at Teotihuacán and Tula and, centuries later, Tenochtitlán. Even in the selection of the site different criteria from those traditionally favored in central Mexico seem to have prevailed (Fig. 26).

The ascent to the main square from the south is one of the finest accomplishments of pre-Columbian urban designers and is as worthwhile an experience as the long walk along the main axis of Teotihuacán. The climax is a large regular square surrounded by a low wall which permits magnificent north and south views to the valley far below, in contrast to the sense of being enclosed which the constructions to east and west provide.

El Tajín (Fig. 27) is contemporary with Xochicalco, and the two cities reached their peak of development at the same time. El Tajín is located some three hundred kilometers northeast of Teotihuacán but in a completely different environment—the humid, steamy coast of the Gulf of Mexico north of the area that witnessed the development of Olmec culture centuries before. There is no doubt that the Totonecs of El Tajín maintained contact with the classic centers of central Mexico, of the Petén, and Yucatán, but they kept intact a stone architecture and sculpture of great originality.

The ruins of El Tajín are not as well known as those of other classic centers. They cover an extensive undulating surface with few flat areas, so that the city had to be built at different levels. The builders took advantage of one flat section to construct several groups of buildings around regular squares climaxed by the famous Pyramid of the Niches (Fig. 28). These groups constitute the lower level, possibly one of the earlier stages of the city. No over-all design for the whole seems to have existed. Centuries later, the builders of El Tajín started terracing the slopes of a neighboring hill located to the north of the initial site. While the buildings on the lower level had a religious function, civic and religious uses were combined in those constructed on the slopes and at the top of the hill. It is precisely in this broken terrain that totally different principles of architecture and urban design were employed, as exemplified by the extensive use of terraces and stairways, the appearance of informal and irregular arrangements and a subtle use of topograhy—all pointing to a closer relation with the Mayan world.

Monte Albán was settled during the formative period. It was one of the more continuously occupied pre-Columbian centers. During the first millennium A.D. it was a highly influential center in Middle America, and the capital of the Zapotecs. The core of Monte Albán was its Great Square, one of the most beautiful open spaces ever conceived by man (Fig. 29). The square was developed over the centuries on top of a hill that had been flattened out to provide a surface of some 400 by 200 meters, and was completely surrounded by temples and "palaces." The conception of the Great Square of Monte Albán is a flexible one, incorporating the monumental axiality of the ceremonial centers of central Mexico with the free disposition and the architectural elements of the Mayas (Fig. 30). Any expansion of the Great Square was limited by the natural possibilities of the site. The fronts of the buildings face the square, leaving no openings toward the valley that surrounds the hill on three sides; they provide a sense of total enclosure and a detachment in relation to the topography and environment that is quite unique in Middle America. With the passage of time the architecture of the Square suffered periodic changes but its general proportions apparently remained the same.

The city itself grew unplanned on the slopes of the main hill and on the neighboring hills. There is little doubt about the large size and population of Monte Albán; however, no general layout has been discovered, and everything indicates a settlement with the physical characteristics of a Mayan center—although possibly with a higher density of population—rather than with the very urban characteristics of contemporary Teotihuacán or of the post-classic centers of central Mexico.

Urbanistically, Tenochtitlán passed through two stages. The first commences with the founding of the city on an island near the southwest shore of Lake Texcoco in the year 1325 A.D. and with the founding of Tlatelolco two years later by another group of Aztecs; it terminates with the reign of Montezuma I (Fig. 31). The second stage lies between the reign of Montezuma I and the conquest of the city by the Spaniards in 1521 A.D. During the first decades, in fact for almost its first century, Tenochtitlán was a modest village whose huts were constructed of poles, mud, and *zacate* (fibrous straw). Gradually, as the Aztecs established themselves more firmly, both militarily and politically, the city extended across the shallow waters surrounding the original islands. The effort and patience employed must have been enormous. The expansion of the city demanded the construction of canals in whose midst were intensively cultivated *chinampas* or floating islands. This technique, still employed on the outskirts of Mexico City, consists of forming artificial banks of very fertile soil out of the natural vegetation and mud of the locality.

The elementary social structure of the Aztecs when they established themselves on the islands of Lake Texcoco after years of wandering was apparently adequate for their initial construction projects. However, about 1367, they decided for reasons of prestige to elect a king. Their choice fell upon Acamapichtli, a prince of Culhuacán and a descendant of the Toltec dynasty. Acamapichtli, commenced a line of succession which lasted a century and a half and crowned eight kings by the time Cortés arrived. Little by little, Aztec society acquired a hierarchy, and the kings increased their power and took upon themselves the attributes of a deity until, under Montezuma II, complete temporal and spiritual control was in the hands of the king. In this manner a governing class was established, responsible for

34

all military, religious, judicial and administrative affairs, enjoying numerous privileges which commenced at infancy when the children of the aristocracy were sent to the *calmecac* or school to learn "good habits, doctrines and exercises and to lead a hard and chaste life" (Sahagun, 1938). War and religion were the preferred careers, as they led to the prestige and honors to which the Aztecs aspired.

Tenochtitlán grew rapidly and its fortunes swelled with the expansionist development of the Aztec state whose political and military capital it was, as well as being the religious and cultural center. It is possible that the Aztec state was just reaching its territorial limits when the arrival of Cortés and his men supervened. Aztec development had perforce to take place within the areas already under Aztec domination and could be achieved only through an effort to increase production, as few territories of any economic or stategic importance, from which tribute could be exacted, remained to be conquered.

Tenochtitlán depended for its existence on tribute and trade, and through the riches so acquired it was able to support a large population occupied exclusively with governmental, religious, cultural, or military pursuits. Among the powerful groups in the city were the merchants, who were of great importance in its development and in the political and economic consolidation of the Aztec state. The products of the whole of Middle America were exchanged in the market of Tlatelolco (which was the busiest) and in that of Tenochtitlán, while the work of the Aztec craftsmen, in turn, was transported on the backs of bearers as far as Xoconuchco, on the west coast of Guatemala, or to the Laguna de Terminos on the coast of the Gulf of Mexico, where trading took place with the Mayas of Yucatán.

The Aztec doctors, architects, and sculptors had attained remarkable sophistication. Aztec doctors performed trepanning and puncture operations on the skull and successfully treated bone fractures. The sculptors executed monumental works, some with a complex symbolism such as the figure of Coatlicue, the Earth Goddess (which is to be seen in the Mexico City Museum), others of an extraordinary realism and dignity, such as the famous Head of the Eagle Knight. The number of craftsmen must have been large and varied, the metal and feather workers and the stone carvers producing work of outstanding quality. The populace on the lowest level of society became ever more widely separated from the privileges of the governing classes, although they were not slaves. Their integration into the society was effected by means of the *calpulli* or clan, which meant a certain guarantee of survival. At the very bottom of the social scale were the

35

slaves, a large group made up of prisoners of war, lawbreakers, and the indigent.

Aztec society was urban; its institutions and social classes were for that time and region intensively urban in character, having an economy based on trade, tribute, and specialized crafts. Tenochtitlán was a symbol of success. Without doubt it was the most advanced example of urban life in pre-Columbian America. Montezuma I was the fifth king of the Aztec line and reigned between 1440 and 1468. He conquered the Totonec territory on the Gulf Coast and expanded the Aztec state to Oaxaca. By the end of his reign, all the peoples of sub-areas I, II, and III, with the exception of a few small pockets, were under his military or tributory domination. Montezuma I instituted a form of jousting or knightly combat, called in Spanish "la guerra florida," to test the valor of the warriors and to take the prisoners required as human sacrifices to the war god Huitzilópochtli, adopted a short time earlier as the creator deity of the Aztecs. But Montezuma I was also responsible for laying the groundwork of the city that so amazed the Spaniards in 1519. We may assume that with his reign the village stage of Tenochtitlán ended and the construction of the great city commenced, coinciding with the first expansion of the Aztecs and their allies beyond the central Mexican plateau. With the assistance of Netzahualcoyotl, the great Poet-King of Texcoco, an aqueduct which brought water from Chapultepec to the center of Tenochtitlán was constructed, and a dike was built some sixteen kilometers long to protect the city from floods and from the excessive salinity of Lake Texcoco, which would have been harmful to the cultivations of the *chinampas*. Montezuma I also brought in a group of architects from Chalco who transformed the architecture of the city within a few years.

The basic plan of Tenochtitlán was cruciform (Figs. 32–33). The two axes crossed the center of the city at the Great Temple, where there was the maximum concentration of religious buildings, and divided the city into four districts. In each district there were various wards, each with its temples, squares, markets, general constructions and schools (Vaillant, 1962). It is possible that the cruciform plan of Tenochtitlán originated during the reign of Itzcoatl, the fourth monarch of the dynasty, when the Aztecs commenced to build the causeways which permanently connected the still precarious island sites with the mainland of the lake. The Spaniards make mention of three causeways which, commencing at the center of the city, went northwards toward Tepeyacac, westwards toward Tlacopán, and southwards toward Ixtapalapa and Coyohuacán (Fig. 31). These three causeways coincided with three gateways in the walled enclosure surrounding the Great Temple. A fourth causeway following an easterly direction ended at the eastern bank of the island, where there was a landing place for the canoes that carried passengers and cargo to other cities situated around the periphery of Lake Texcoco.

There is no doubt that the basic cruciform plan influenced the orientation of the streets and canals which formed the primary transit network of the city, and that gradually an original and obviously intentional layout developed (Fig. 34). The cruciform plan was also repeated in other cities of the Mexican central plateau.[20] At the intersection of the two causeways, not far from the point where the Aztecs constructed the first temple of the city in honor of Huitzilópochtli, there arose with the passing of the years the great Teocalli or Great Temple of Tenochtitlán. The Great Temple had the external shape of a square (Fig. 35). On each of the four sides—420 meters in length—that formed the limits to the sacred precinct, there was a wall decorated on the outside with the heads of hundreds of plumed serpents. Within the enclosure there were eighteen main structures and groups of buildings, as well as a number of smaller ones. The most important edifice was the pyramid that served as a pedestal for the twin temples consecrated to the worship of Huitzilópochtil and Tlaloc.[21] Other important buildings were the round-based temple with a conical roof dedicated to Quetzalcoatl, and the ball-court; both were placed on the same east-west axis as the Great Pyramid. The prolongation of this axis through the western gate of the sacred enclosure became the Tlacopan or Tacuba causeway.[22] In the interior of the sacred precinct was the school or *calmecac*, and on the exact spot where the Cathedral of Mexico City now stands there was a temple dedicated to the sun (Figs. 36–37).

The layout of Tenochtitlán lacks the precision of that of Teotihuacán. Upon an original, spontaneous pattern, certain regulatory criteria were superimposed which gradually gave rise to a relatively orderly plan for the city. Furthermore, although the monumentality of the Great Temple was obviously calculated, judging by the scale of its separate constructions and their concentration within a restricted area, the refinement and perfect progression of Teotihuacán is absent. Without doubt Tenochtitlán was the dynamic capital of an expanding state in continuous transformation. Within the brief span of their existence, its rulers and artists were never able to complete their work.

EARLY ATTEMPTS AT URBAN PLANNING IN SOUTH AMERICA

Contemporaneously with Teotihuacán a culture flourished to the south of Lake Titicaca which from the year 150 A.D. had its regional center in Tiahuanaco. The valley of Tiahuanaco was already inhabited during the formative period. It is a longish valley, with soils of poor quality, which runs from east to west and is flanked by two ridges of hills, now much eroded and with deep fissures. The hills on the north side of the valley separate it from Lake Titicaca and from Chiripa, a center inferior only to Tiahuanaco in importance in the region. The site of Tiahuanaco is twelve kilometers from the lake and 35 meters above the level of its waters.

The flowering of Tiahuanaco took place between the years 150 and 360 A.D. The principal constructions and the design of the center date from this period. It is a design without known antecedents in the region. The presumably urban area is of rectangular shape measuring three kilometers in length by one in width. To the south and east of the limits of possible urbanism, platforms were discovered which may have been the entrances to the city. Although they are believed to date from a later period, there may have been other previous constructions on the same spots contemporary with the three principal ones. No platforms have been found on the north or east sides. The location of the south platform coincides with the prolongation of the axis separating the pyramid (Akapana) and the temple (Kalasasaya).[23] Up to now there is no conclusive evidence about the layout and urbanistic characteristics of Tiahuanaco, if Tiahuanaco was really a city in terms of the criteria I have adopted.

Tiahuanaco was constructed of mud-brick (adobe) and stone. The constructions prior to the flowering, as well as the civic buildings, were made of mud-brick. In the construction of the ceremonial edifices, as in the small semi-underground temple (Fig. 38), red sandstone from the hills to the south of the city was used. Andesite was much less used, due to its rarity in that vicinity. The origin of the andesite used in the Puerta del Sol (Gateway of the Sun) and in the Ponce monolith was probably on the far shore of the lake. With this information it is not easy to determine precisely the functions of Tiahuanaco and its urban characteristics. "The exact nature of the great site of Tiahuanaco is still uncertain, although to judge by its size and the presence of remains over wide areas, it may well have been a large village and not a city."[24]

The political and social prerequisites of a governing elite, and its planning sense, are evident in Tiahuanaco. If this were not so, works on such a scale, using materials brought from considerable distances, could not have been carried out, nor would there have been any point in the monumental effect produced by the design of the ceremonial centers. On the other hand, there is no evidence that the design of Tiahuanaco was repeated in other centers of the same culture or that there was any attempt anywhere in that presumably urban area to organize its layout. More difficult still is the task of determining the functions carried out in Tiahuanaco. The ruins of a still unexcavated structure to the east of the urban area alongside the east-west axis may be those of a "palace." Only few remains of dwellings have been found. The lack of confirmation of any residential function at Tiahuanaco may be due to the particular stress given to the researches carried out there; but there is just as much uncertainty about the town's political, administrative, and commercial functions, if any. There is no doubt, however, that Tiahuanaco was a religious center of great prestige for that time and region, and that it was persistently utilized for centuries. It may have been this prestige which induced the governing elite to design and construct the first ceremonial center planned on a monumental scale in the southern highlands.

Those who know Teotihuacán and Tiahuanaco and analyze them from the viewpoint of urbanization may find some interesting points of comparison. The first is that Tiahuanaco is less monumental in scale and design; second, that the conception of Tiahuanaco is more simple and primitive, while its architecture and sculpture are less refined; third, that the sculpture of Tiahuanaco is more rigid and static; lastly, that its architecture is not so well finished.

If, on visiting Tiahuanaco and commencing with the small sunken temple—the only one reconstructed (Fig. 38)—one analyzes the relation between the temple and the nearby enclosure of the Kalasasaya, it immediately appears that both groups were conceived on an axial criterion and that an intentional bilateral symmetry function was set up on an axis which, passing through the eastern gateway of access to the Kalasasaya, unites the central stela of the temple with the Ponce monolith. Utilizing the stela as a pivot and turning round 90° to the south, another axis at right angles to the former leads with considerable exactitude to the center of the access stairway to the small sunken temple (Fig. 39). This, in turn, is at right angles to the principal axis of the whole of the central group of Tiahuanaco, by which is meant the axis or roadway running east-west and dividing the Kalasasaya on the north from the Pyramid or Akapana to the south.

These two structures, the most important of this sector of the center, have a similar orientation.

However, the over-all urbanistic organization would not have been the same. The east-west axis and a north-south axis at right angles to it—the length and characteristics of which have not been precisely established—were utilized as a device for freely arranging the principal masses. None of the principal structures corresponds axially to either of them. The two axes do not give the impression of having been determining elements in locating the constructions, but of having been traced out later to introduce some kind of order into the movement toward the ceremonial center.

The flowering of the regional states along the coast of Peru was evidenced by the population growth, the remarkable craft specialization and technological progress, especially in metalwork, and the expansion of militarism. Intensive agriculture supported by irrigation systems and fertilizer was fully developed by then.[25] Stylistically it was the period of the famous Mochica and Nazca pottery on the northern and southern coasts respectively. The realistic designs ornamenting Mochica pottery leave no doubt as to the existence of a militarily supported state exercising strong social and political control over one or more valleys. The expansion of the Mochica state was one of the great regional political experiments on the coast during that period, although it was confined to the northern valleys with an extension southwards that may have reached the Santa River valley.

The preoccupation of the authorities with enlarging the irrigated area and raising the general standard of living of the people is reflected in the great utilitarian constructions of this period which, in some of the coastal valleys, such as the Virú, has been called "the golden age" (Willey, 1953). The little valley of the Virú is the best known of those on the northern coast. The Virú valley was incorporated into the Mochica state during those centuries and into other states in subsequent centuries, so that its urbanistic development may serve to illustrate the urbanization process in the valleys of the north coast. In Virú this was evidently a period of demographic growth and of expansion toward the middle and upper valleys, although many of the sites which were inhabited during the formative period remained occupied. It is not yet possible to speak of urban planning. The majority of the population lived in small villages developed haphazardly.[26] The population density in those sectors of the valley seems to have been much higher and its economy more diversified and insured by sizable irrigation projects, but these concentrations do not seem related to any clear principle insofar as location and interrelation are concerned. It is surprising that a society organized in this manner and capable of such vast projects of regional infrastructure did not show equal urbanistic capacity or preoccupation. There are no indications that any capital existed in the Virú valley or in the neighboring, broader valleys of the Chicama and the Moche, which were the dispersion centers of the Mochica culture. The fight for the control of arable land was no doubt at the bottom of the policy that gave rise to military operations, but the urbanistic and architectural vacuum in a society so advanced in other ways is surprising.

The appearance of true cities in South America occurred when the first millennium A.D. was already well advanced, in other words several centuries later than this development in Middle America. To judge from the scale of the coastal centers and the functions of Tiahuanaco, they could not have possessed the characteristics of true cities during the flowering of the regional states.

The appearance of cities on the coast coincides with the expansion of the Tiahuanacan horizon, whose dispersion center seems to have been an extensive but little-known site in the central highlands called Huari, some twenty-five kilometers to the north of the present-day city of Ayacucho. In Huari a cult appears to have been established, having the support of a vigorous military movement which united the valleys of the coast as far north as the Lambayeque valley under some form of control and brought the regional classic states to an end.

Urbanistically it is a period of great interest, not only because of technological innovations and the scale of some of the new centers but also because of the appearance, possibly for the first time in the sub-areas of South America under analysis, of a purposeful urban systemization using elements which could be adapted to different urban scales (e.g., El Purgatorio, Fig. 42). In two of the northern coastal valleys which have been analyzed in detail, similar principles seem to have been repeated which correspond to the hypothesis mentioned. A survey of the valley of Casma located two large cities, one small city, a cluster of four enclosures, and five examples of small isolated buildings, whose construction would have commenced during the Tiahuanacan period.[27] The larger of the two big cities "is made up of numerous platforms, courtyards, rooms, and passages. It is regular and planned, and in some places the walls are decorated with geometrical friezes or niches."[28] The ruins cover an area of $27\frac{1}{2}$ hectares, while that of the isolated buildings never exceeded one hectare. It is interesting to note that in the single structures a distribution of chambers and courtyards appears, made with mud-brick (adobe) and using cornerstones, which seems to be repeated in the larger-scale buildings, naturally with greater elaboration of layout, constructional devices and ornamentation.

In the Virú valley, as in the other valleys of the northern coast, the expansion of the Tiahuanacan horizon was characterized by a general state of unrest. In the low part of the valley two large enclosures having very high walls were constructed, coinciding with the consolidation of farming zones nearer to the coast. The population may have continued to increase within these large enclosures, and at some point one of them must have served as the valley's admininistrative center.

These large enclosures are subdivided into a few vast compartments; there are also smaller ones which have only a few small chambers. The interior courtyards and the galleries are characteristic, and in some there are "small platform-like mounds." The arrangement of the chambers in every enclosure was much more orderly than in the villages of previous periods.

The Tiahuanacan expansion established the criteria for urban regulation on the coast which were to prevail during subsequent periods. If this expansion was backed up and afterwards maintained by the military and had sufficient power to do away with highly developed styles such as the Mochica, it may be logically thought that the regional classic states had, in one form or another, been incorporated into a system of government with a higher degree of centralization and power. This power and centralization may have been exemplified in two valleys, the Casma and Virú, by intense building activity and by the incorporation of new techniques.[29] The construction work included roads connecting the valleys, new irrigation canals and, possibly for the first time, those sunken cultivation grounds called *pukios* which are characteristic of the northern coast. Furthermore, the greater part of the population of Virú seems to have concentrated in the high valley, following a tendency which had begun to appear during earlier periods. All these represent very significant changes in the life of these valleys, which would indicate the influence of an elite with power to make decisions and with a sense of total innovation. In other valleys of the central and southern coasts, which are not so well known archaeologically, cities were built which show some of the criteria of urban systematization already mentioned with respect to the northern valleys. The most outstanding examples of this period are those of Pachacamac (Fig. 41), whose origin dates from before the Tiahuanacan expansion on the central coast, and La Centinela, on the south coast (Fig. 40).

THE GOLDEN AGE OF URBANIZATION
IN SOUTH AMERICA

Toward 1000 A.D., Tiahuanacan influence on the coast had lost its importance. During the period which followed, new states were formed along the coast: the Chimú in the north, the Cuismancú in the center, and the Chincha in the south. It was also a period of more intense urbanization along the coast.

On the northern coast the Chimú Empire extended southward as far as the central coastal valleys.[30] Its southern frontier seems to have been marked by the impressive fortress of Paramonga, one of the best examples of pre-Columbian military architecture (Figs. 43–44).

The Chimú capital was Chan Chan, located in the wide valley of the Moche a few kilometers to the north of Trujillo, one of the first Spanish cities in Peru. The ruins of Chan Chan cover an area of some twenty kilometers, extending to the shores of the Pacific. No coastal city prior to Chan Chan was of such a scale. The actual archaeological zone covers less than a third of this area and is almost entirely occupied by eleven citadels which constitute a peculiar characteristic of Chan Chan, and by intermediate spaces. The layout and internal structure are very different from that which prevailed among the classic and post-classic cities of central Mexico and the Maya area. Nevertheless, Chan Chan seems to represent the culmination of the urbanistic ideas that existed on the northern coast of Peru after the Tiahuanacan expansion.

Chan Chan seems to have been an unplanned grouping of standardized elements designed in accordance with uniform criteria (Fig. 45). For this reason I consider that Chan Chan is the culmination of a process which developed on the northern coast on the basis of ideas probably originating outside the area. The repetition of the same elements, although with a different intensity of utilization, is noticeable in all the citadels, and the uniform orientation of all except one of them—19° east of north— is evidence of preconceived criteria. The standardization of the elements themselves and their interrelationship, as well as the similar dimensions of the squares and chambers, provide further proof that Chan Chan was not an urbanistic innovation but a more mature and finished example of centuries of empirical experimentation.

What has already been said about the larger city of the Casma valley [Chapter VI, p. 41] was also valid for other cities of the northern coast during the post-Tiahuanacan period. In each citadel the same disposition of the streets is repeated, following a regular right-angled pattern, with regularly shaped squares and small chambers laid out in line. In all or nearly all the enclosures, unbuilt areas known as *canchones*, the *pukios* and the pyramids, or *huacas*, repeated themselves (Figs. 46–49).[31] The walls are high, solid, and almost entirely without doors (Fig. 50). What varied was the utilization of land. For example, the *canchones* represent 39.6% of the area of the Bandelier citadel but only 9.6% of the Rivero citadel (Figs. 48–49); the external walls with their peripheral corridors covered 27.6% of Rivero and 4.0% of the Laberinto citadel (Figs. 46–47); the *pukios* cover only 1.1% of the Uhle citadel and 9.2% of Tschudi; the rooms or chambers serving as living quarters cover 13.3% of the Uhle citadel and 28.4% of Tschudi. The total areas were also very different. Uhle had an area of approximately 196,300 square meters; Laberinto of 148,500 square meters (Fig. 46), Bandelier of 125,000 square meters, Tschudi of 109,450 square meters and Rivero only 72,750 square meters (Fig. 48).

Up to the present it has not been possible to determine what the functions of these citadels were, or the reasons for constructing such high walls, or who lived within them. It is even more difficult to establish the precise reasons for the differences in the intensity of land use.

Various authors have endeavored to find an answer to these questions. It has been suggested that the population was split up for municipal and social reasons,[32] that the walls were built to impede movements of population,[33] that the citadels represented subdivisions or clans of the Chimú society,[34] that within a given city the inhabitants were grouped according to specialty,[35] or that each citadel was the residence of a chieftain with his immediate servitors.[36] None of these theses has been supported by researches in depth. I am inclined to believe, bearing in mind the repetition of the same urban and architectural elements and the same constructional techniques, that all the citadels fulfilled similar functions, and that if they served as permanent residences they were occupied by groups with by and large the same social status (Fig. 51). The problem of finding an explanation for the high walls almost or totally devoid of openings is still more intriguing, but beyond our scope.

Between the citadels there were some built-up areas. I do not know if these areas were prior or subsequent to the citadels or were constructed and occupied simultaneously with them. The examination of a recent aerial photograph reveals a repetition of the same arrangement of progressions of small chambers and regularly shaped squares as is found in the interior of the citadels. However, it is not apparent, nor does it seem possible in view of

44

the disposition of the citadels and the constructions in the intermediate areas, that one or more avenues existed that crossed the city or linked up the citadels. The communications within the city were no doubt effected by narrow streets running like alleyways between walls, but there does not seem to have been any predetermined general layout. The city appears to have grown by the addition of repetitive elements wherever its burgeoning demanded. It is possible that the citadels were the initial components, since each of them shows a high degree of internal organization affecting a relatively extensive area and maintaining a similar orientation in all or nearly all cases. Moreover, it would have been more difficult to form the *canchones* in areas previously built upon. If this hypothesis is correct, then the intermediate areas would have been occupied either almost simultaneously or later, in any case only after the limits of the citadels had been defined.

An intensification of the urbanization process also took place on the central coast. A representative example of this is Cajamarquilla, a site of considerable extent, unfortunately in a very bad state of preservation (Fig. 52). Cajamarquilla must have been contemporaneous with Chan Chan. Architecturally and urbanistically it had many aspects in common with the capital of the Chimú, although the high walls are absent. The construction is of brick or adobe molded by means of wooden forms, but the ruins have deteriorated to such an extent that no signs of a general layout are discernible. Narrow alleys between the dwellings undoubtedly existed, but there are no wide streets to be seen. Nevertheless, the characteristic courtyards, rooms, platforms and *huacas* of other coastal cities were repeated.

The expansion of the Inca Empire and of Cuzco, its capital city, took place simultaneously. Up to the fourth decade of the 15th century, Cuzco was a small town exercising little influence over others similar to it in the region, but beginning in the reign of Pachacuti, the ninth Inca in the line of succession, the construction of the Empire commenced. The Empire was the work of Pachacuti, a great conqueror and statesman who ruled between 1438 and 1471, and of his son Topa Inca Yupanqui, who reigned between 1471 and 1493. In little more than half a century the limits of Inca rule had reached their maximum expansion. Concomitantly with the military expansion, vast programs of land recuperation, colonization, and road and storehouse construction were undertaken.[37] The organization of the Empire was the idea of Pachacuti, who integrated the peoples under a centralized rule as soon as they were conquered. Furthermore, the cult of Ticci Viracocha, the Creator, was imposed upon the conquered states; they were permitted to retain their tribal gods, but only as secondary deities.

The growth of Cuzco was undoubtedly a consequence of the greater political influence and the administrative requirements of an empire undergoing expansion. The change and the gradual development of the center of Cuzco toward another site situated some hundreds of meters to the north of the original location, as well as the remodeling of the Inca capital, resulted from measures taken by Pachacuti. Possibly these were the outcome of a desire to create an image of the new power in the land, and at the same time to build a better city with the wealth from tribute.

Despite its symbolic character and its political-administrative nature, and despite the power and the wealth which the Incas had at their disposal from the time of Pachacuti onwards, Cuzco never managed to typify urbanization. It lacked the commercial activity of Tenochtitlán, the monumentality of Teotihuacán, and the elaboration of Tikal—nor would it seem that Cuzco had the scale or the population of Chan Chan. The reports of the first Europeans who visited the Inca capital and the few studies which exist on pre-Hispanic Cuzco indicate that it was not even particularly outstanding among the urban centers of the Inca rulers.

The Incas made use of the cities they conquered. Some of them like Quito, Tumibamba, Tumbez, Chan Chan, Cajamarca, Pachacamac, Vilcas and others, were state capitals or regional centers which the Incas conquered and remodeled to meet their own needs and programs. They also founded cities in regions where there were no centers suitable for the administrative functions on which the Incas based the success of their undertakings and the hegemony of their empire, as for example Pumpu and Huanuco. The wars of conquest brought about the construction of new towns like Incahuasi; and the colonization and consolidation of new territories made necessary the creation of new centers such as Viracochapampa, Ollantaytambo and Machu Pichu, Choquesuysuy and the numerous small centers of the Urubamba basin.

Shortly after the arrival of the Spaniards at Cuzco it was split up and divided among the conquerors. In a few decades the physiognomy of the city changed. The great Inca square was reduced to less than a fourth of its size, churches replaced the Inca religious constructions, and many fine walls of hewn stone belonging to the palaces of the erstwhile lords of Cuzco were used as foundations for the large houses of the conquerors. The layout of the Cuzco of the Incas is still partially in existence (Fig. 53). The two principal axes of the city crossed on the square, their extremities extending in the direction of the four regions into which the empire was divided. The line taken by the axes was far from being straight, nor did the city have "streets in the form of a cross," as Pedro Sancho (1962) (Fig. 54) has pointed out. The topography would have made this difficult. Nevertheless, it is evident that some order existed in the general disposition. The image of the Tahuantisuyu, the Inca empire, was intentially repeated in the layout of the suburban districts, inhabited by people from the four quarters of the territory.

The heart of Cuzco was its Great Square, the Huacapata, formed by two sectors separated by the canalized bed of the river Huatanay. To the north of the river, where the "Plaza de Armas" stands today, there was a sector known as Aucaipata reserved for the Inca nobility and dedicated to the ceremonies over which the Inca himself (the emperor) presided from a platform, or *usno*. To the south there was an expanse more than three times larger which was called Cusipata, known today as the Plaza de Regocijos or Square of Joy, where military parades and festivities for the populace were held. The shape of the Great Square was that of two large trapezoids united at their smaller bases, and it had an area of over 12 hectares (Fig. 55). The palaces of Viracocha Inca, Huayna Capac and other Incas, and certain other special buildings, were built north of the Huatanay, surrounding or near the Great Square.

Urbanistically, Cuzco lacked the monumentalism of other contemporary cities in Middle America. If, as one author suggests, "Pachacuti's intention seems to have been to construct a ceremonial center having a cluster of small groupings around it," one understands why only a small area of the city, formed by the palaces, temples and administrative buildings surrounding the square, possessed urban characteristics and densities.[38] The builders of Cuzco made no attempt, either, to take advantage of differences in level to obtain varying effects. The design of the center was simple. The imposing frame of the surrounding mountains was the only contrast with a city of sober stone architecture and narrow streets (Fig. 56).

A number of the cities founded or utilized by the Incas are known. None of them, with the exception of Machu Pichu, has been studied in detail. As Machu Pichu is far from representing the urbanistic ideas of the Incas, it is difficult for the time being to establish precisely which criteria were followed by a government whose public works were often long-term projects. I am inclined to believe that a society which dedicated such efforts to constructing an efficient regional infrastructure would have developed urban criteria for the building of new cities. The displacements of populations for political and economic reasons would doubtless have benefited from the repetition of a proven urban model. All societies that colonized new territories as the result of decisions by a central government, as occurred during the Hellenistic period and, some centuries afterwards, during the expansion of the Roman Empire, adopted standard criteria for urban layouts which they applied to the new cities. The Incas may also have done this, in which case the criteria would have been in line with those adopted in the construction of inns, or *tambos*, or in the marking and defenses of the roads or in the construction of storerooms, or *colccas*.

The Inca cities were not fortified, although some of them had fortresses a short distance away as a means of protection (Fig. 57). There is one element common to all Inca cities, and that is the square, or plaza. The Inca square was of large dimensions and regular shape, although none is identical with another. I have already mentioned that the Great Square of Cuzco was the result of two trapezoids united at their smaller bases. Ollantaytambo had two plazas, an internal one, slightly trapezoidal, within the city proper, and another square-shaped one surrounded by structures on all four sides, on the opposite bank of the river Patacancha, where the *andenes* or terraced walks and principal buildings are to be found. The plazas of Pikillacta were also square-shaped—this site being a storage center of possibly pre-Inca origin (Fig. 58)—as were those of Viracochapampa (Fig. 60). The plaza of Tambo Colorado is an irregular trapezoid. The square of Pumpu was trapezoidal, open at the west side. That of Huanuco Viejo was an imperfect rectangle measuring approximately four hundred by six hundred meters, having its principal accesses at the corners and a construction in the center (Fig. 59). That of Vilcas-Huaman, the most important city between Cuzco and Jauja, was an immense regular polygon. The square of Jauja "is large and has a quarter of a league" comments a chronicle.[39] On the other hand, the square of Machu Pichu was irregular, although spatially it may appear to be an immense rectangle. Bordered by walls, its shape is adapted to the promontory on which the city was constructed. The regularity of the Inca squares may also have been imposed on cities captured and remodeled by the Inca administration.

These squares must have had a variety of functions. They were nearly always traversed by the Inca Road which connected all the principal cities of the Empire (Fig. 61). A recent study of the square of Huanuco Viejo supports the supposition that justice was administered from the structure or *usno* found in its center.[40] There is no doubt that the squares were the scene of public festivities and functions organized by the Inca hierarchy or its regional delegates. The square was also a meeting place and a center for commercial transactions based on barter.

1. Map of Middle America and South America showing location of most intense urbanization.

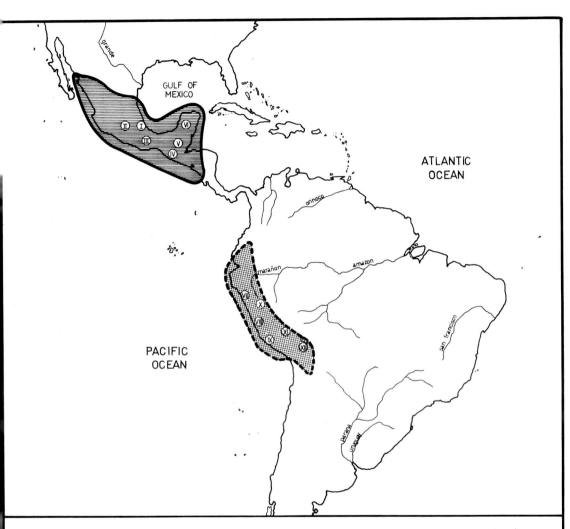

MIDDLE AMERICA AND SOUTH AMERICA: LOCATION OF THE TWELVE SUB-AREAS

 MIDDLE AMERICAN CULTURE AREA
AREA OF MOST INTENSE URBANIZATION IN PRECOLUMBIAN SOUTH AMERICA

2.

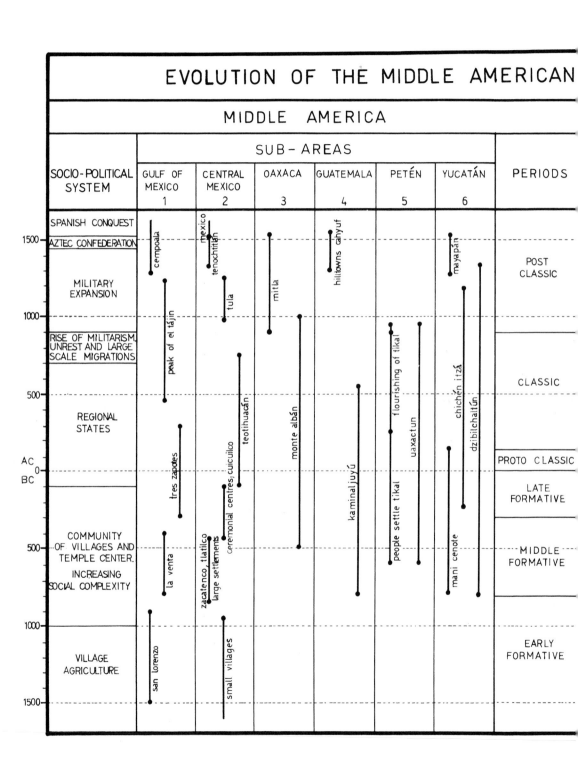

EVOLUTION OF THE MIDDLE AMERICAN

MIDDLE AMERICA

SOCIO-POLITICAL SYSTEM	SUB-AREAS						PERIODS
	GULF OF MEXICO 1	CENTRAL MEXICO 2	OAXACA 3	GUATEMALA 4	PETÉN 5	YUCATÁN 6	
SPANISH CONQUEST	cempoala	mexico tenochtitlan		hilltowns cahyuf		mayapán	
AZTEC CONFEDERATION							POST CLASSIC
MILITARY EXPANSION	peak of el tajin	tula	mitla				
RISE OF MILITARISM, UNREST AND LARGE SCALE MIGRATIONS		teotihuacán			flourishing of tikal	chichén itzá	CLASSIC
REGIONAL STATES	tres zapotes	ceremonial centres, cuicuilco	monte albán	kaminaljuyú	uaxactun	dzibilchaltún	
							PROTO CLASSIC
					people settle tikal		LATE FORMATIVE
COMMUNITY OF VILLAGES AND TEMPLE CENTER. INCREASING SOCIAL COMPLEXITY	la venta	zacatenco, tlatilco large settlements				mani cenote	MIDDLE FORMATIVE
VILLAGE AGRICULTURE	san lorenzo	small villages					EARLY FORMATIVE

AC 0
BC

1500
1000
500
500
1000
1500

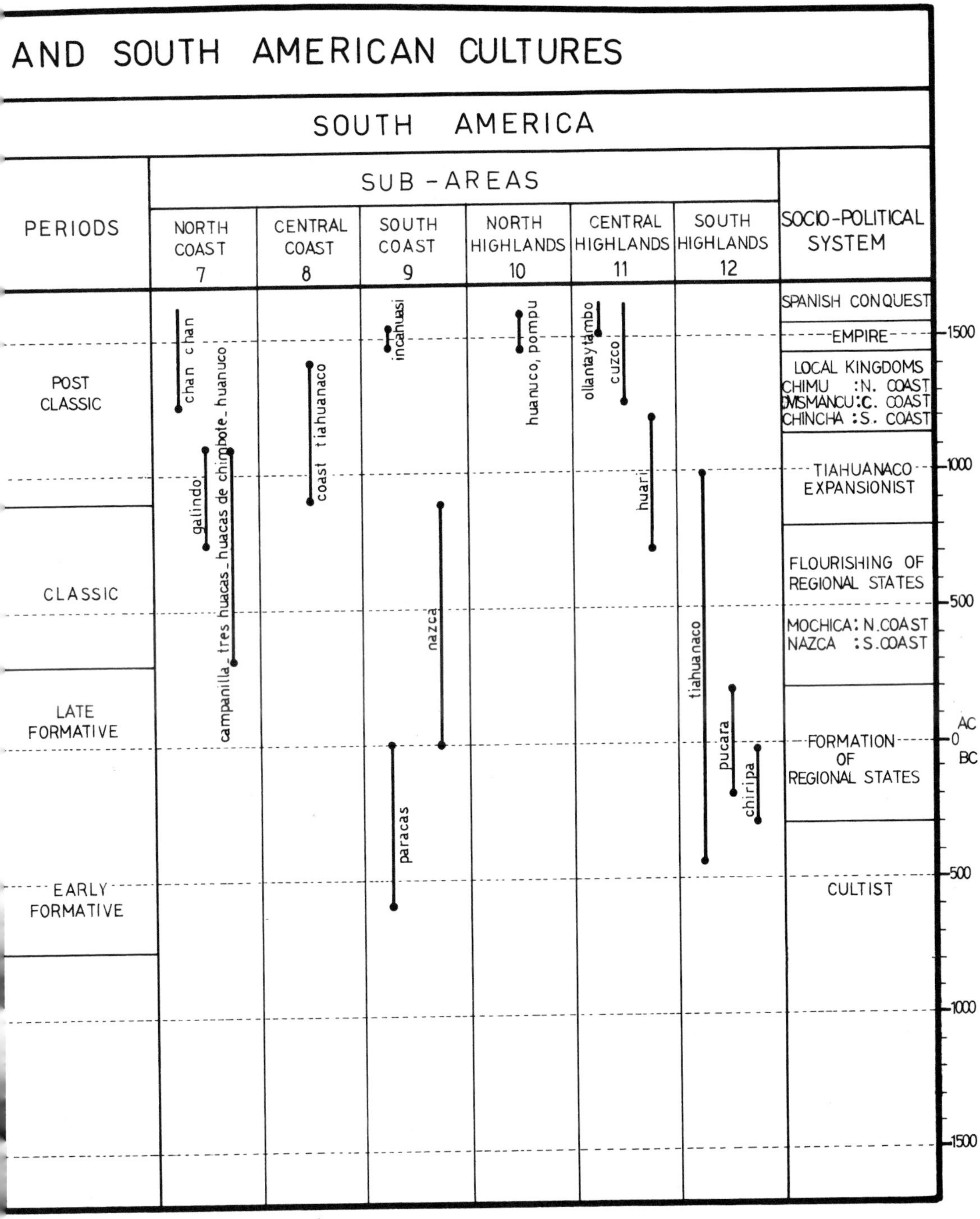

AND SOUTH AMERICAN CULTURES

SOUTH AMERICA

PERIODS	SUB-AREAS						SOCIO-POLITICAL SYSTEM
	NORTH COAST 7	CENTRAL COAST 8	SOUTH COAST 9	NORTH HIGHLANDS 10	CENTRAL HIGHLANDS 11	SOUTH HIGHLANDS 12	

Culture labels (by column):

- **North Coast (7):** chan chan; galindo; campanilla_tres huacas_huacas_huacas de chimbote_huanuco
- **Central Coast (8):** coast tiahuanaco
- **South Coast (9):** incahuasi; nazca; paracas
- **North Highlands (10):** huanuco, pompu
- **Central Highlands (11):** ollantaytambo; cuzco; huari
- **South Highlands (12):** tiahuanaco; pucara; chiripa

Periods (left column): POST CLASSIC; CLASSIC; LATE FORMATIVE; EARLY FORMATIVE

Socio-political system (right column):
- SPANISH CONQUEST
- EMPIRE
- LOCAL KINGDOMS
  - CHIMU : N. COAST
  - CWSMANCU : C. COAST
  - CHINCHA : S. COAST
- TIAHUANACO EXPANSIONIST
- FLOURISHING OF REGIONAL STATES
  - MOCHICA : N. COAST
  - NAZCA : S. COAST
- FORMATION OF REGIONAL STATES
- CULTIST

Time scale (right): 1500, 1000, 500, AC 0 BC, 500, 1000, 1500

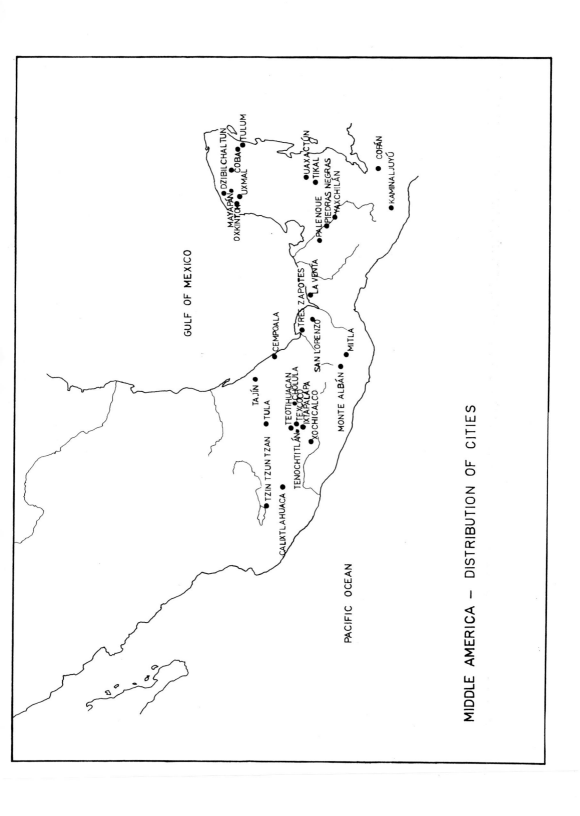

GULF OF MEXICO

TULUM
COBÁ
DZIBILCHALTUN
UXMAL
MAYAPÁN
OXKINTOK

UAXACTÚN
TIKAL
PIEDRAS NEGRAS
PALENQUE
YAXCHILÁN

COPÁN

KAMINALJUYÚ

TRES ZAPOTES
LA VENTA

CEMPOALA

SAN LORENZO

TAJÍN

TULA

TEOTIHUACAN
TEXCOCO
CHOLULA
TENOCHTITLÁN
IXTAPALAPA
XOCHICALCO

TZINTZUNTZAN

CALIXTLAHUACA

MONTE ALBÁN

MITLA

PACIFIC OCEAN

MIDDLE AMERICA – DISTRIBUTION OF CITIES

3. Map of Middle America showing location of principal cities mentioned in the text.

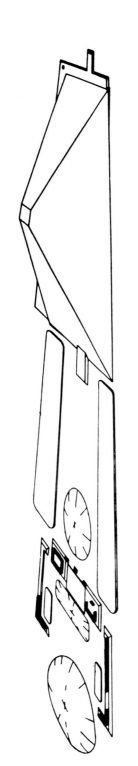

4. La Venta, c. 800 B.C. Reconstruction of the Ceremonial Center, according to Drucker, Heizer, and Squier.

5. Teotihuacán. General map of the central zone of the city, showing cruciform plan and location of the principal constructions. (See note on page 116.)

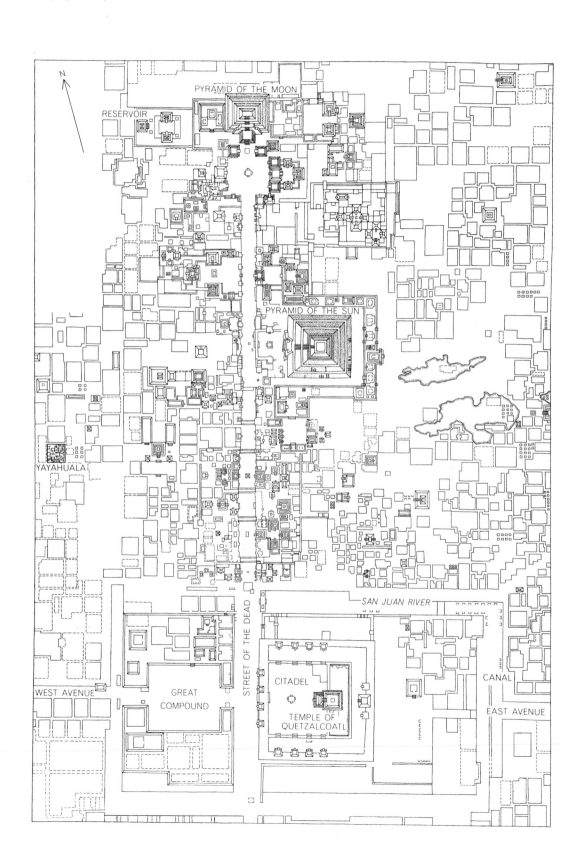

N

PYRAMID OF THE MOON

RESERVOIR

PYRAMID OF THE SUN

YAYAHUALA

STREET OF THE DEAD

SAN JUAN RIVER

CANAL

WEST AVENUE

GREAT COMPOUND

CITADEL

TEMPLE OF QUETZALCOATL

EAST AVENUE

6. Teotihuacán, c. 0–400 A. D., aerial view of the excavated zone. Along the axis is the Calle de los Muertos (Street of the Dead) ending at the Pyramid of the Moon. In the middle, to the right of the street, is the Pyramid of the Sun. Below and to the right, the Citadel. Compare with Fig. 5.

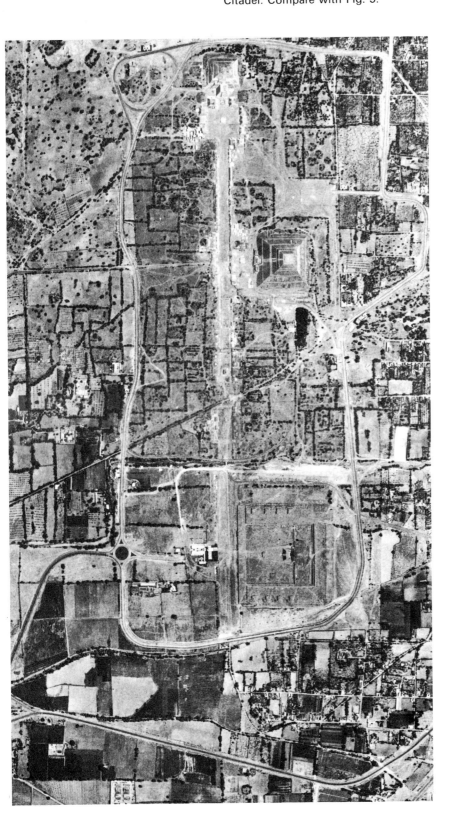

7. Teotihuacán. View of the Street of the Dead, with the Pyramid of the Sun at right and the Pyramid of the Moon at center (July, 1961).

8. Teotihuacán. Ruins of the Viking group, one of the "palaces" bordering the Street of the Dead. The sunken level of the street should be compared with the level of the "palace." (See note on page 116.)

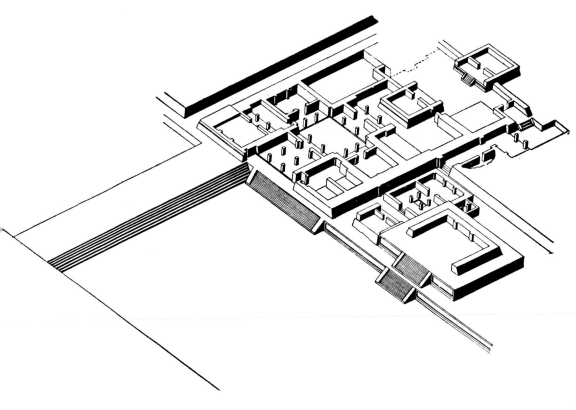

9. Teotihuacán. The Citadel (La Ciudadela). In the foreground the San Juan River. Note the group's perfect symmetry and sober architecture.

10. Tikal. General plan of the ruins, c. 900 A. D. The plan covers an
    area of 16 square kilometers (about 6 square miles). The map is
    divided into 500-meter squares. The dwellings were built to
    avoid low-lying ground. (See note on page 116.)

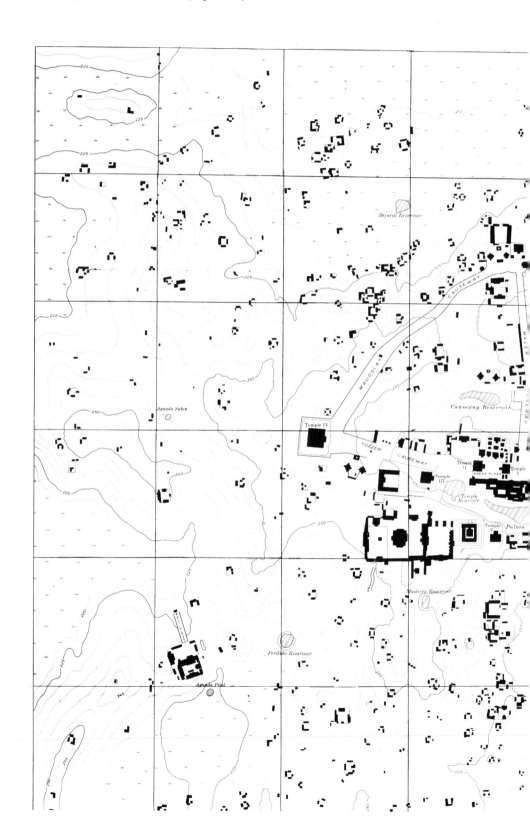

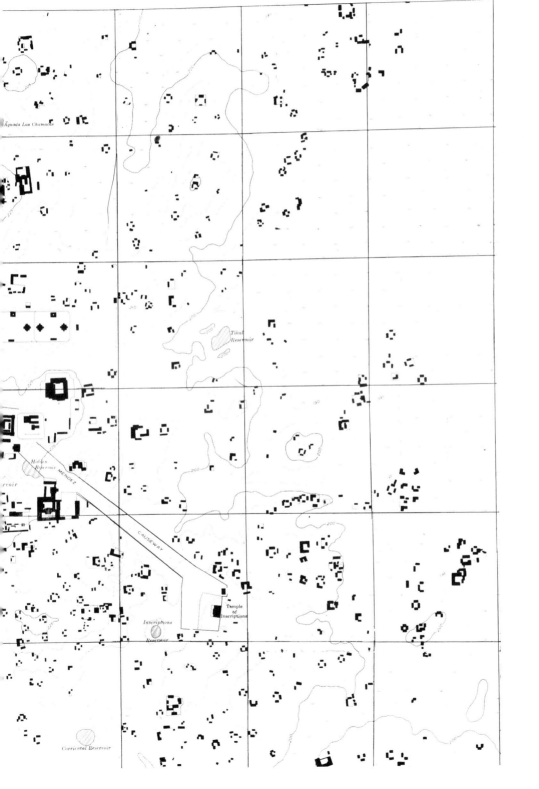

Aguada Las Chamacas

Tikal
Reservoir

Hidden
Reservoir

MENDEZ

CAUSEWAY

Temple
of
Inscriptions

Inscriptions
Reservoir

Corriental Reservoir

11. Plan of the central zone of Tikal. (See note on page 116.)

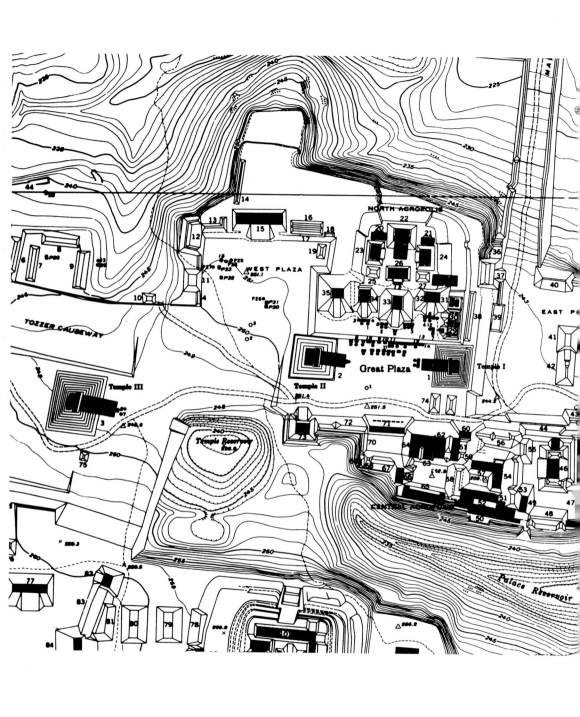

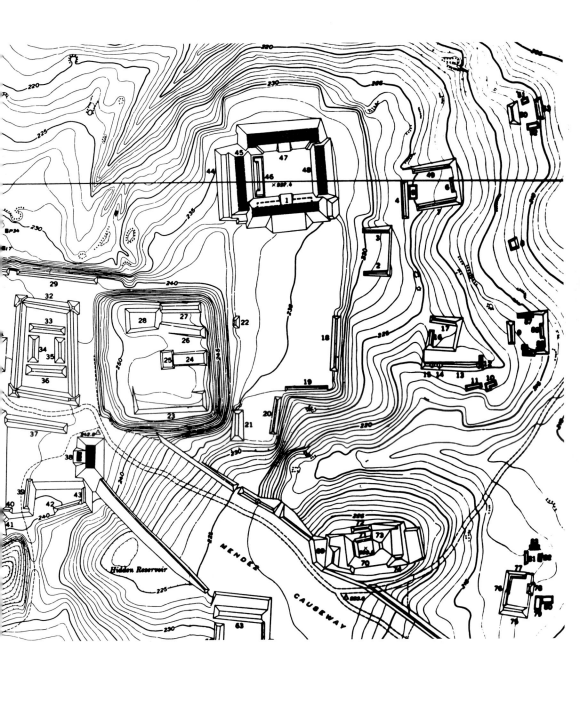

12. Tikal. Air view of the jungle closing on the center of Tikal.

13. Tikal. Recent view of the Great Plaza of Tikal. In the foreground Temple I, to the right the North Acropolis, and in the background Temple II.

14. Palenque. View of the ruins (July, 1961). To the right, the Palace with its three-storied tower

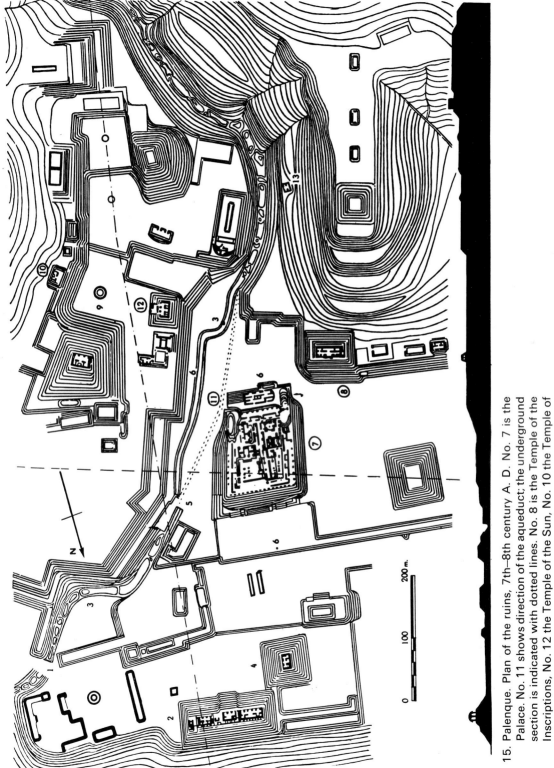

15. Palenque. Plan of the ruins, 7th—8th century A. D. No. 7 is the Palace. No. 11 shows direction of the aqueduct; the underground section is indicated with dotted lines. No. 8 is the Temple of the Inscriptions, No. 12 the Temple of the Sun, No. 10 the Temple of the Foliate Cross.

16. Yaxchilán. Plan of the ruins of one of the most flourishing Maya centers in the Usumacinta River valley at the end of the classic period, 7th–8th century A. D.
17. Piedras Negras. Reconstruction of the Acropolis north of the western group plaza.

18. Piedras Negras. Plan of the ruins, 7th–8th century A. D. Topography was of fundamental concern in the location of the groups of buildings and the conformation of the plazas.

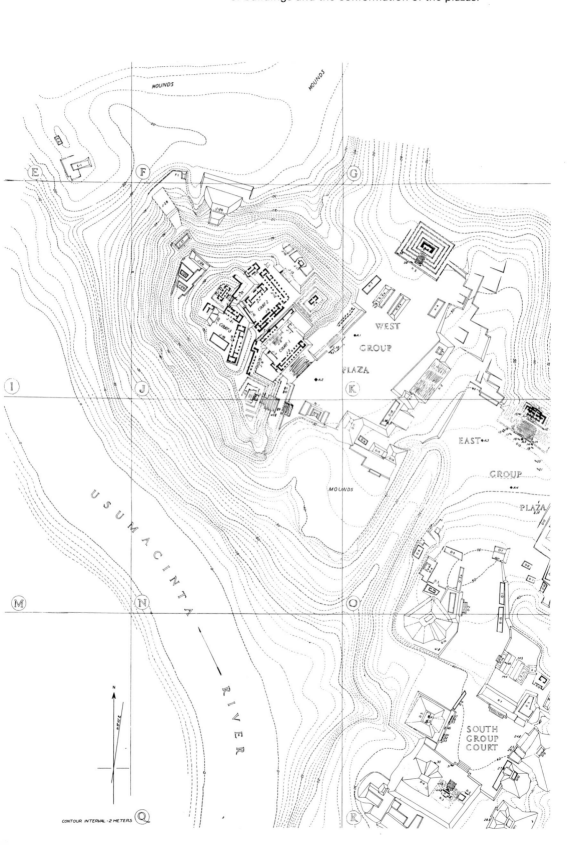

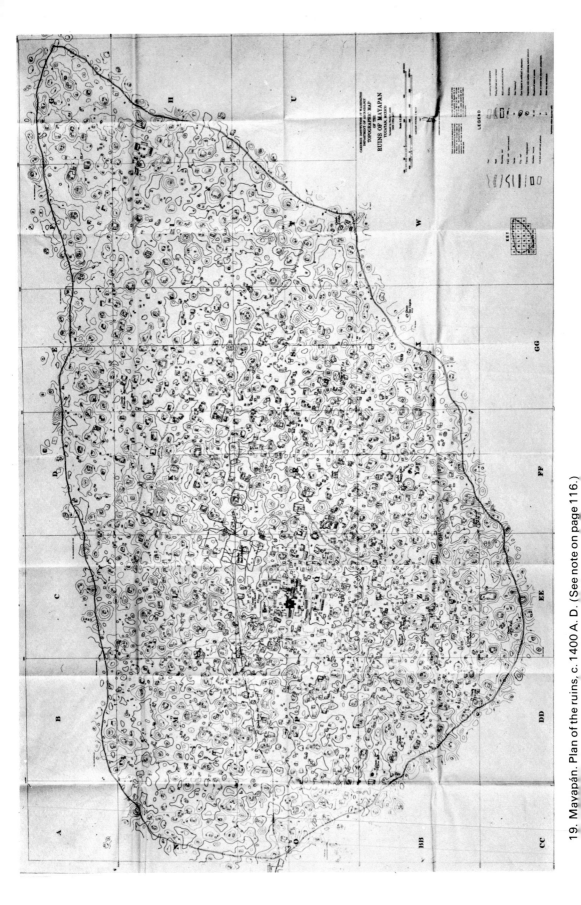

19. Mavapán. Plan of the ruins, c. 1400 A. D. (See note on page 116.)

20. Uaxactún, 7th–8th century A. D. Plan of the ruins.

21. View showing the location of Tulum on the top of a rocky cliff on the east coast of the Yucatán peninsula. In the center, the ruins of El Castillo (The Castle). 11th—15th century A. D.

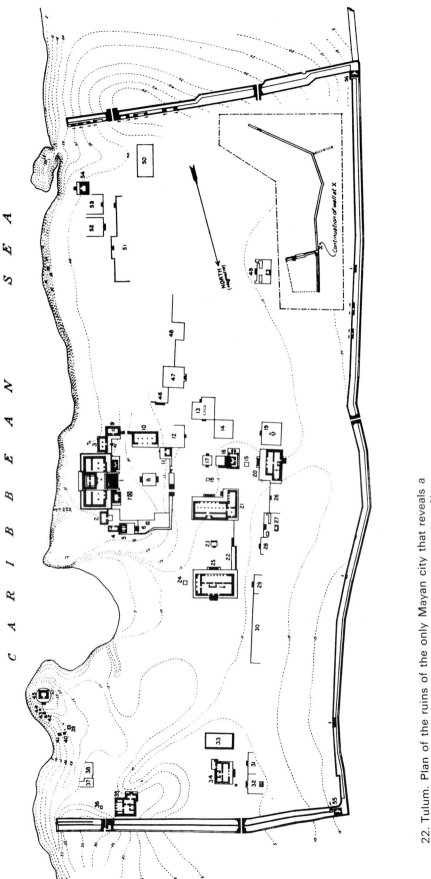

22. Tulum. Plan of the ruins of the only Mayan city that reveals a purposeful urban arrangement in straight parallel streets. Note disposition of the constructions on both sides of a street linking the gateways of the north and south walls.

C A R I B B E A N   S E A

NORTH (magnetic)

Continuation of wall at X

23. Air view of Tula, the Toltec capital, 10th–13th century A. D. Tula was the principal city of central Mexico during the centuries between the decline of Teotihuacán and the flowering of Texcoco and, afterwards, Tenochtitlán.

24. General view of the square of Tula (July, 1961). Note that the famous *atlantes* have been placed on the upper terrace of the pyramid, at left.

25. Xochicalco. Plan of the ruins, 5th–13th century A. D. "P" is the
    upper square with the building of the Plumed Serpent (M) in the
    center. Access to the square is from a long uphill street from (S),
    having a series of terraces.

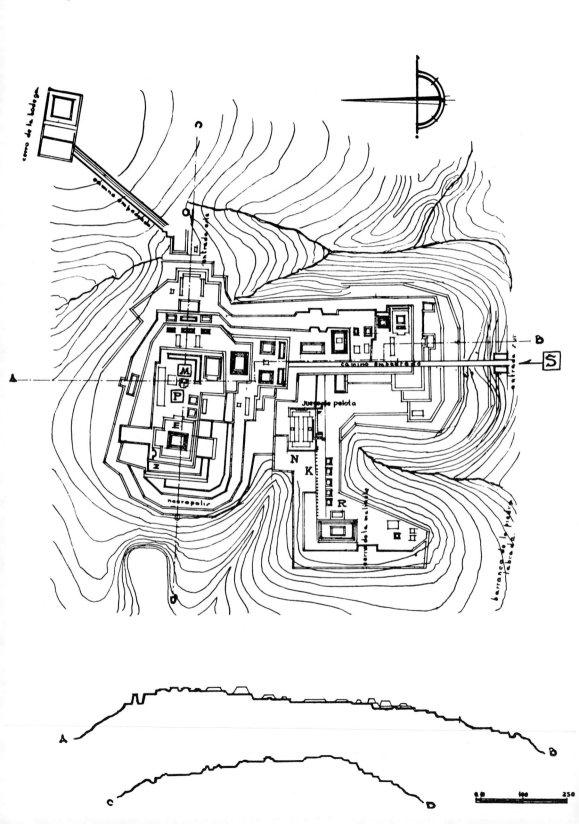

26. Xochicalco. Aerial view of the ruins from the west. Observe how the constructions totally cover the principal hill and the neighboring one of La Bodega.

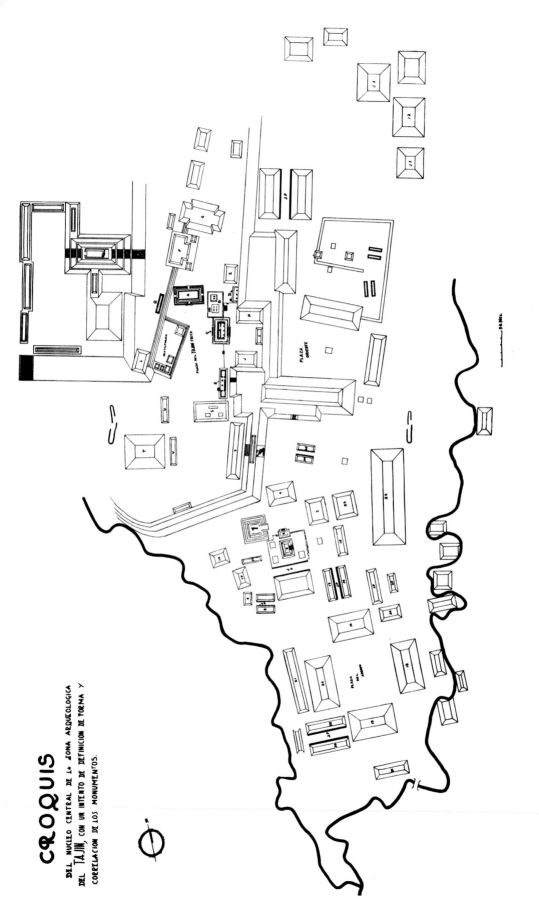

CROQUIS

DEL NUCLEO CENTRAL DE LA ZONA ARQUEOLOGICA DEL TAJIN, CON UN INTENTO DE DEFINICION DE FORMA Y CORRELACION DE LOS MONUMENTOS.

PLAZA DEL TAJIN CHICO

PLAZA ORIENTE

PLAZA DEL ARROYO

27. El Tajín. 5th–13th century A. D. Plan of the ruins. The city was constructed at various levels not indicated on the plan. No. 1 is the Pyramid of the Niches.

28. El Tajín. The Pyramid of the Niches seen from the north (July,1961).

29. Monte Albán. Aerial view of the main square, first millennium A. D. The city extends over a group of hills. Above left, the ball court. Right, the staircase giving access to the principal pyramid. Left, the north platform.
30. Monte Albán. Photograph of the square taken from the north platform (July, 1961).

31. The valley of Mexico and surrounding country at the time of the Spanish conquest, c. 1520. Lake Texcoco provided an excellent means of communication and trade and in the area developed the most important urban system of central Mexico during the two centuries before the conquest.

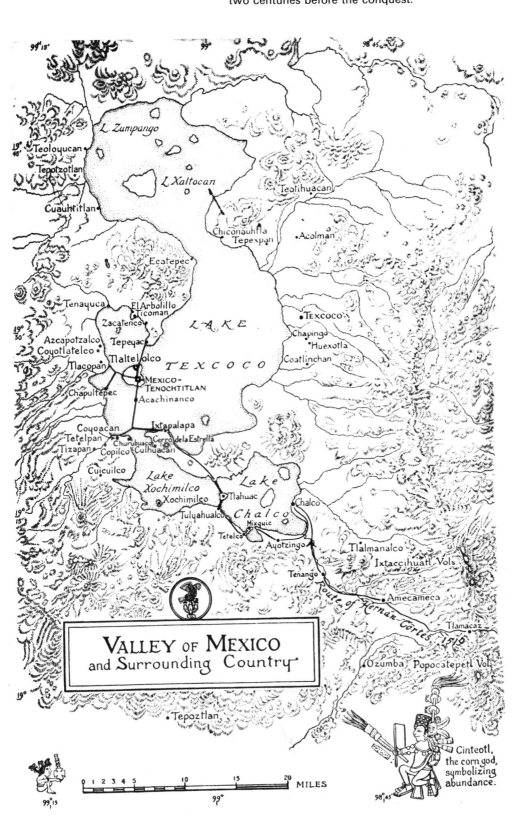

VALLEY OF MEXICO
and Surrounding Country

Cinteotl, the corn god, symbolizing abundance.

0 1 2 3 4 5   10   15   20 MILES

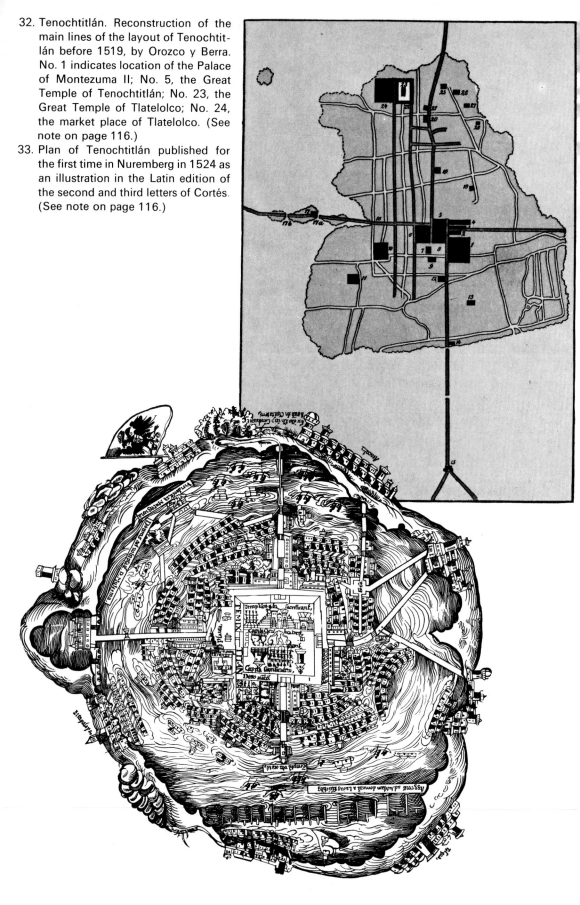

32. Tenochtitlán. Reconstruction of the main lines of the layout of Tenochtitlán before 1519, by Orozco y Berra. No. 1 indicates location of the Palace of Montezuma II; No. 5, the Great Temple of Tenochtitlán; No. 23, the Great Temple of Tlatelolco; No. 24, the market place of Tlatelolco. (See note on page 116.)

33. Plan of Tenochtitlán published for the first time in Nuremberg in 1524 as an illustration in the Latin edition of the second and third letters of Cortés. (See note on page 116.)

34. A 16th century plan on maguey (century plant) paper drafted
several decades after the conquest, which shows a *chinampas*
sector to the north of the Great Temple of Tenochtitlán (indicated by large seated figure at bottom) and some hundred meters to the east of the Great Temple and market of Tlatelolco
(open rectangle at top). Roads are indicated by a double line;
canals by a wavy line between straight lines.

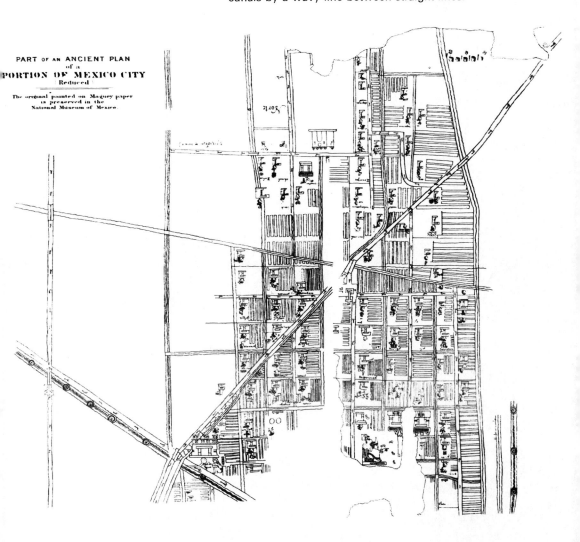

PART of an ANCIENT PLAN
of a
PORTION OF MEXICO CITY
(Reduced)

The original painted on Maguey paper
is preserved in the
National Museum of Mexico.

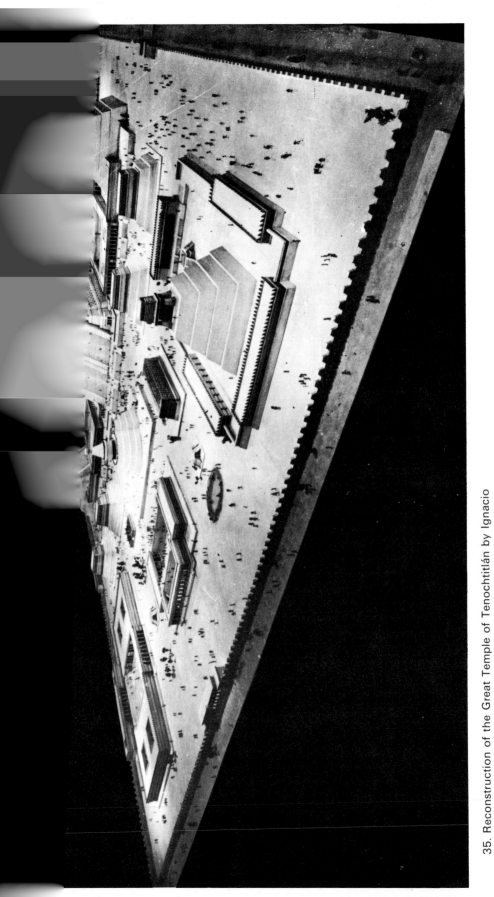

35. Reconstruction of the Great Temple of Tenochtitlán by Ignacio Marquina. In the right foreground the Temple of the Sun, in the middle foreground the ball court, and at left corner the *calmecac* or school. The twin temples of the principal pyramid were dedicated to Huitzilópochtli and Tlaloc. The round-based pyramid in the center served as a base for the temple of Quetzalcoatl. Compare with Fig. 36.

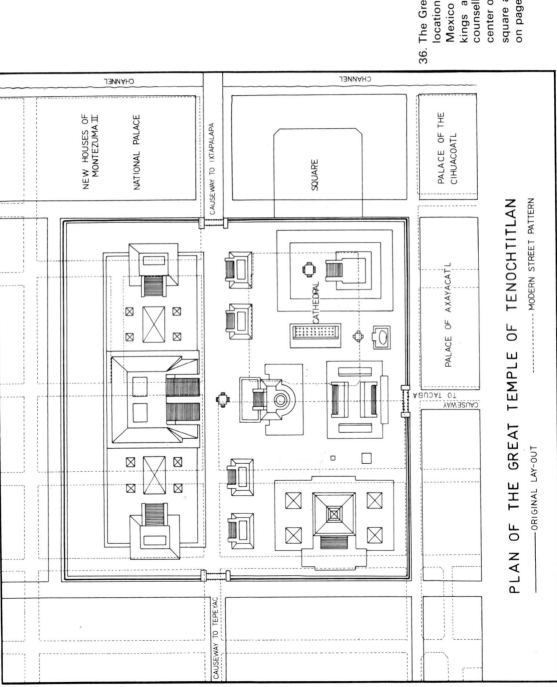

PLAN OF THE GREAT TEMPLE OF TENOCHTITLAN

——— ORIGINAL LAY-OUT

------- MODERN STREET PATTERN

Labels within plan:

CHANNEL

NEW HOUSES OF MONTEZUMA II

NATIONAL PALACE

CAUSEWAY TO IXTAPALAPA

CHANNEL

SQUARE

PALACE OF THE CIHUACOATL

CATHEDRAL

PALACE OF AXAYACATL

CAUSEWAY TO TACUBA

CAUSEWAY TO TEPEYAC

36. The Great Temple of Tenochtitlán and its location in relation to the present layout of Mexico City. The palaces of the Aztec kings and of the *cihuacoatl* (principal counsellor of the king) occupied the center of the city, surrounding the central square and the Great Temple. (See note on page 117.)

37. The buildings of the Great Temple of Tenochtitlán according to an early drawing. In the foreground, from left to right, the *calmecac*, the ball court, and the Temple of the Sun. In the middle, the pyramid of the twin temples. The Great Temple precinct was actually surrounded by a wall and had three doors as indicated here.

Inic vij. parra pho ipan-moteneoa in tle=
in itotoca catca, yoeçerni Macatecolocaleo.

38. Tiahuanaco, 150–360 A.D. View of the small sunken temple from the Akapana (March, 1967). No. 24 in Fig. 61.
39. Tiahuanaco. Entrance to the Kalasasaya enclosure as seen from the small sunken temple.

40. La Centinela. One of the major cities on the southern coast of Peru, in the valley of the river Chincha (Region IX on Fig. 1).

41. Pachacamac. Aerial view of the most important religious center on the central coast of Peru, in the valley of the Lurín River (No. 12 in Fig. 61). The principal religious constructions are at the top of a hill at left, next to the cultivated zone. The Panamerican highway crosses the ruins at right.

42. El Purgatorio. Aerial view of the ruins of one of the key cities of the northern coast of Peru. Region VII on Fig. 1.

43. Aerial photograph of the Paramonga fortress constructed perhaps by the Chimú in the valley of the river Fortaleza on the central coast of Peru (No. 13 in Fig. 61). Note that the neighboring hills are also fortified.
44. Paramonga. View of the north bastion (April, 1967). The Panamerican highway can be seen to the left.

45. Chan Chan. Aerial view of the southern (top photo) and northern (bottom photo) sections occupied by the citadels (No. 14, in Fig. 61). At extreme left (top photo) is the shore of the Pacific Ocean. The view shows that the intermediate spaces between the citadels were built up. The north-south orientation of the citadels is also evident, although no general layout for the city is observable. At the extreme right (bottom photo) is the Huaca del Obispo (No. 1). The Panamerican highway crosses the ruins in the center. (See note on page 117.)

46. Chan Chan. Plan of the "Labyrinth" citadel, represented by No. 8 on the aerial view of the southern sector (Fig. 45). It is one of the citadels with the largest areas dedicated to *canchones*.
47. Chan Chan. Aerial photograph of the "Labyrinth" citadel.

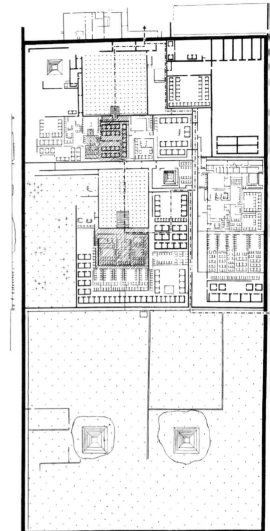

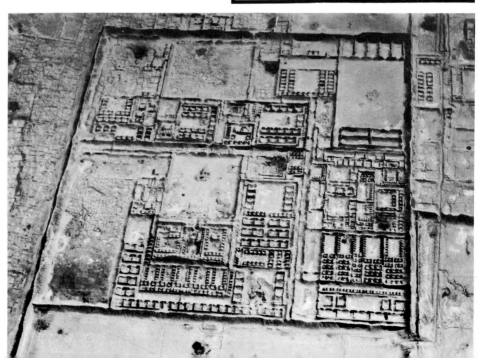

48. Chan Chan. Plan of the Rivero citadel, shown as No. 11 on the aerial view of the southern sector (Fig. 45). The walls of the Rivero citadel are the most imposing of the Chimú capital.

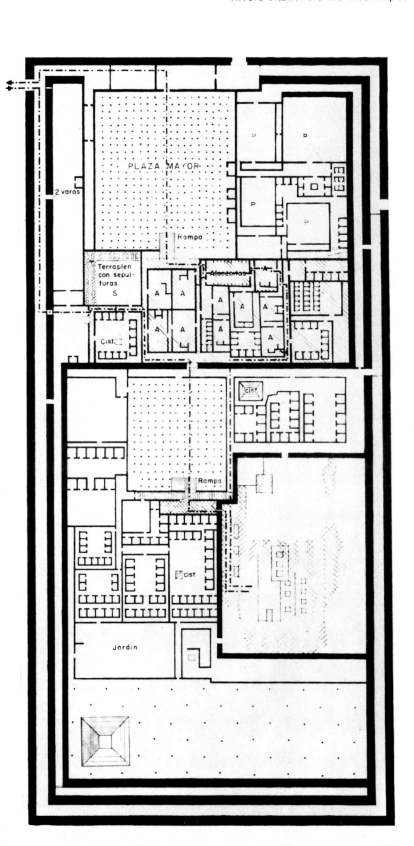

2 varas

PLAZA MAYOR

Rampa

Terraplen con sepul- turas. S

Almacenes

A A A A A

A A A A A

A A

Cist.

cist.

Rampa

cist.

Jardin

50. Chan Chan. View of the outer wall of one of the citadels (January, 1960). The walls were originally higher, but have been eroded by wind and rain.
51. Chan Chan. View of the interior of one of the citadels in which lines of dwellings may be seen (January, 1960).

52. Cajamarquilla. Aerial view of the ruins of one of the most exten-
    sive cities of the Rimac River valley during the postclassic period
    (Region VIII, Fig. 1).

53. Cuzco. Plan of the city in the second half of the 19th century.
(See note on page 117.)

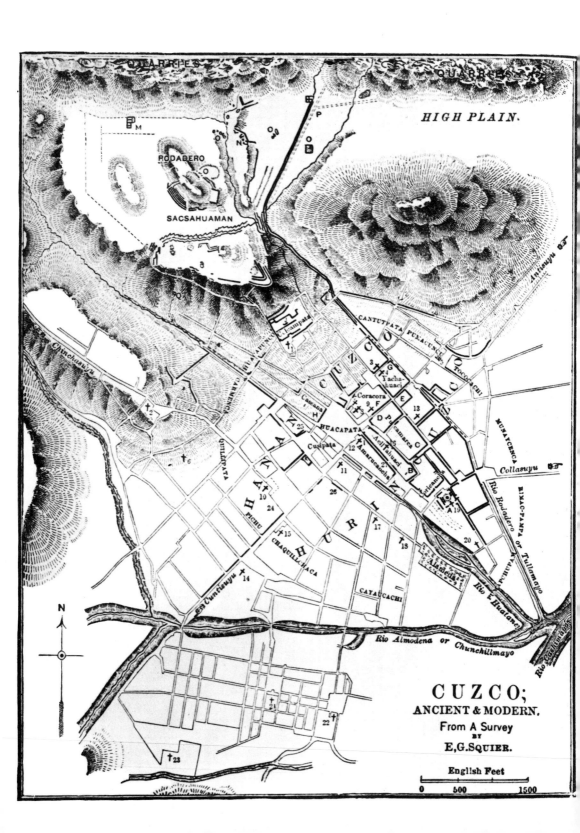

CUZCO;
ANCIENT & MODERN.
From A Survey
BY
E.G.SQUIER.

English Feet

0   500   1500

54. Cuzco. Plan of the city during the colonial period, possibly the 17th century. Note how small the built-up area is. The perfect checkerboard layout is false. Compare with 19th-century plan (Fig. 53).

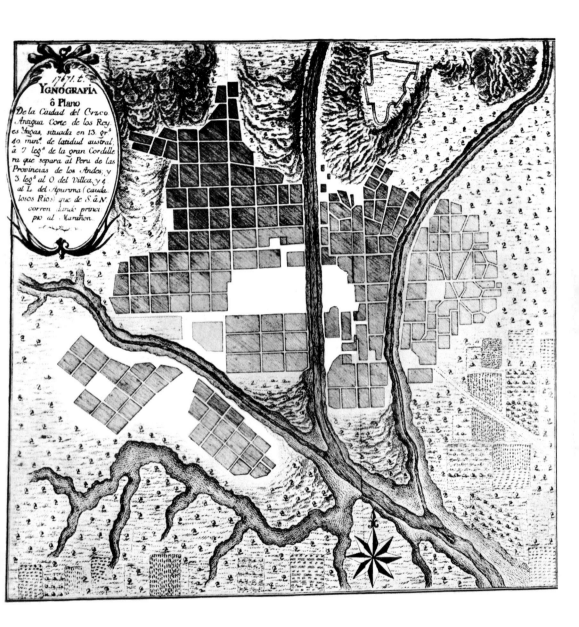

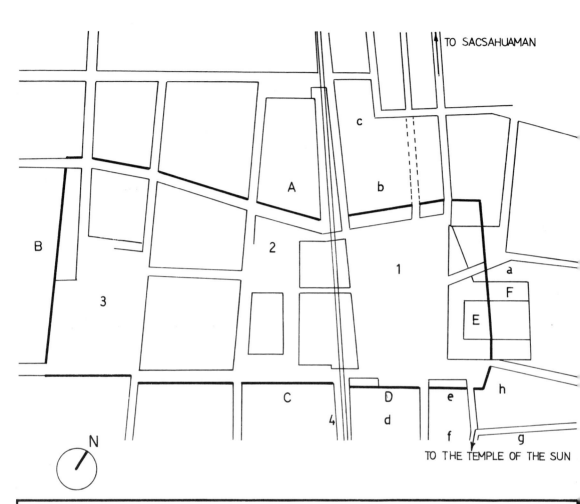

TO SACSAHUAMAN

TO THE TEMPLE OF THE SUN

N

THE SQUARE OF CUZCO BEFORE AND AFTER THE CONQUEST

— LIMITS OF THE INCA SQUARE

0   100   200m

INCA BUILDINGS

a- PALACE OF VIRACOCHA INCA
b- PALACE OF PACHACUTI
c- SCHOOL OF NOBLES
d- PALACE OF AMARUCANCHA
e- PALACE OF HUASCAR
f- PALACE OF THE VIRGINS OF THE SUN
g- PALACE OF TUPAC YUPANQUI
h- HATUM CANCHA
1- AUCAIPATA (PLAZA DE ARMAS)
2-3 SQUARE OF JOY (PLAZA DE REGOCIOSOS)
    AND SQUARE OF SAINT FRANCIS
4- THE CANAL OF THE RIVER HUATANAY

COLONIAL BUILDINGS

A- TOWN HALL
B- SAINT FRANCIS
C- LA MERCED
D- THE UNIVERSITY AND THE
   COMPANY OF JESUS
E- THE CATHEDRAL
F- THE HOLY FAMILY

56. View of an Inca stone wall bordering a city street some 200 meters from the Plaza de Armas (March, 1957). (See note on page 117.)

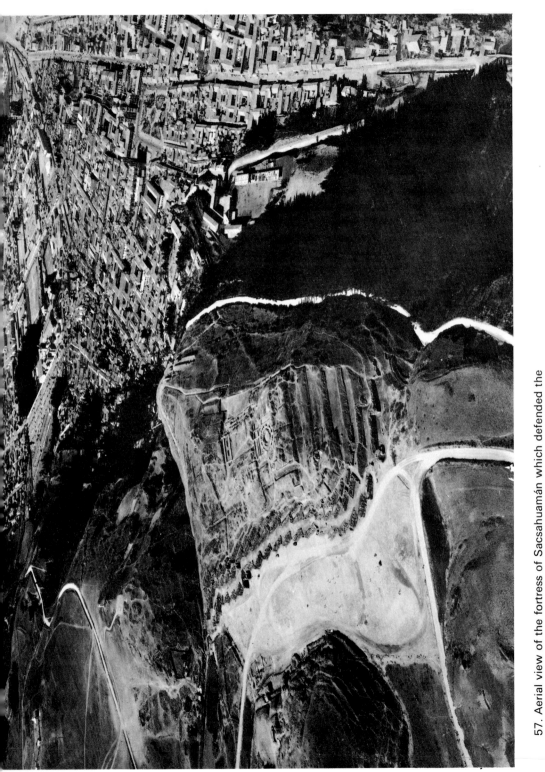

57. Aerial view of the fortress of Sacsahuamán which defended the Inca capital. Observe the triple line of walls next to the central esplanade.

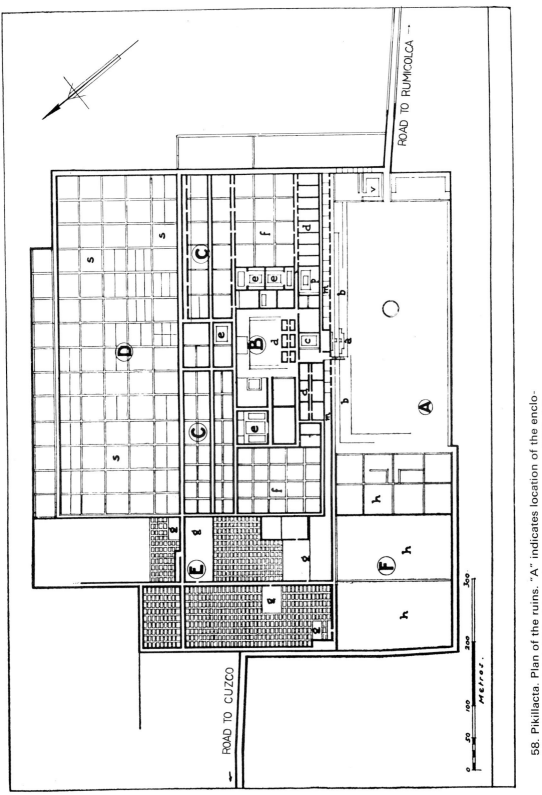

58. Pikillacta. Plan of the ruins. "A" indicates location of the enclosure (canchón), "D" of the colcas or storerooms, and "E" of the storage bins. The dwellings surround the main square "B".

59. Huanuco. Plan of the ruins. (No. 5, in Fig. 61.)

60. Viracochapampa. Plan of the ruins.

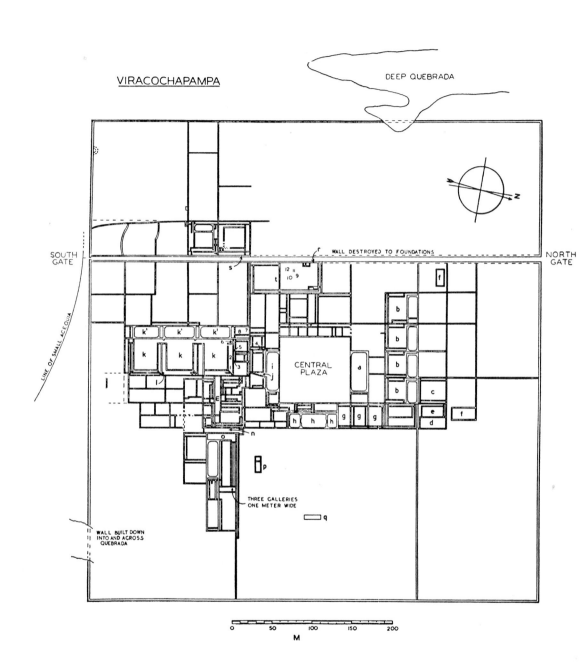

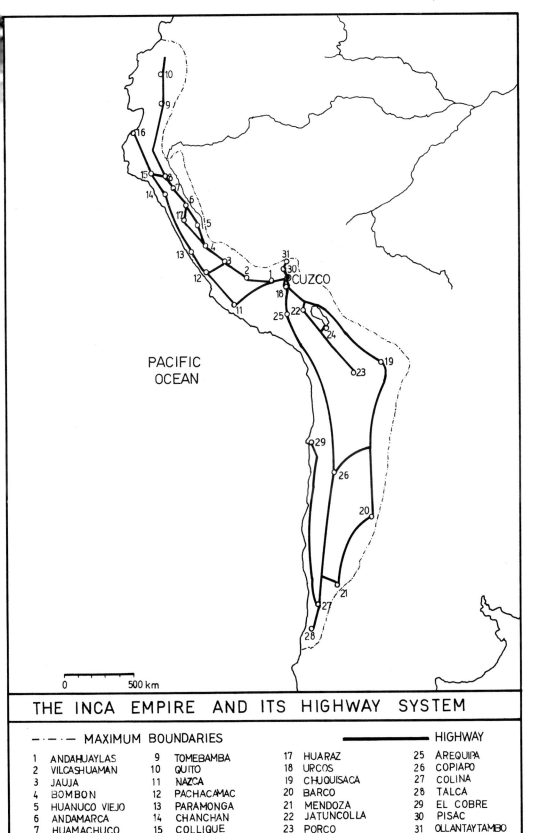

PACIFIC
OCEAN

CUZCO

0   500 km

THE INCA EMPIRE AND ITS HIGHWAY SYSTEM

—·—·— MAXIMUM BOUNDARIES   ━━━━ HIGHWAY

1	ANDAHUAYLAS	9	TOMEBAMBA	17	HUARAZ	25 AREQUIPA
2	VILCASHUAMAN	10	QUITO	18	URCOS	26 COPIAPO
3	JAUJA	11	NAZCA	19	CHUQUISACA	27 COLINA
4	BOMBON	12	PACHACAMAC	20	BARCO	28 TALCA
5	HUANUCO VIEJO	13	PARAMONGA	21	MENDOZA	29 EL COBRE
6	ANDAMARCA	14	CHANCHAN	22	JATUNCOLLA	30 PISAC
7	HUAMACHUCO	15	COLLIQUE	23	PORCO	31 OLLANTAYTAMBO
8	CAJAMARCA	16	TUMBES	24	TIAWANACO	

62. Ollantaytambo. The old Inca city is inhabited to this day. The gridiron of Ollantaytambo is one of the most perfect of those designed by pre-Columbian cultures. (No. 31, in Fig. 61.)

63. Ollantaytambo. Aerial view. In the foreground, the Urubamba
River. The site is halfway up the Patacancha River, which bisects
view. Note how the trapezoidal format of the small township
adapted itself to the site's physical limitations.

64. Machu Pichu. General aerial view of the ruins and of the site from the southeast. The buildings of the hostelry for tourists are at right foreground. The route followed by the modern access road to the ruins from the deep valley of the Urubamba is clearly visible.

65. Machu Pichu. Detailed view of the ruins from the southeast.

66. Machu Pichu. Plan of the ruins.

The feverish building activity of the Incas was doubtless also directed to the creation of new cities, one of whose functions was to unite the various regions of the Empire under one administration.

It is possible that in these new cities, as in the formal organization of their squares, the Inca constructors followed the model of Cuzco. After all, the remodeling of Cuzco and the layout of its square were sponsored by Pachacuti at the initial stage of Inca expansion when none or almost none of the cities mentioned existed, except as mere villages.

If it is correct that the Cuzco model was repeated in the provincial cities, there are reasons for believing that it would have been repeated in Huanuco, an important regional center whose ruins cover an extensive area. Its fine Inca architecture is among the most carefully treated outside of Cuzco. In Huanuco only the square may be considered an urbanistically novel element, and its treatment is simple and functional, although its large size is apparently not in proportion to that of the city. In contrast with the intentional regularity of the square, the street pattern of Huanuco does not seem to have followed any pre-established order, apart from the general sense of direction set by alleyways extending from the sides of the square, and a certain degree of parallelism.

On the other hand, Ollantaytambo, in spite of its small size, is a classic example of Inca urban planning. Its original site was in the valley of Urubamba, some 40 kilometers to the north of Cuzco. A fort existed there which was captured and razed by Pachacuti's armies as a punishment. Shortly afterwards the Inca city was constructed and made an advance post for the defense of the Cuzco valley. The layout of the Inca Ollantaytambo is the nearest approach to that of a gridiron to be found in any of the pre-Columbian cities of South America (Fig. 62). It is divided into two sections cut by the river Patacancha. The fortifications are in the northern section. In the southern section the planned city is to be found. The shape, which is trapezoidal, was determined by the small area existing between the river and the mountain slopes (Fig. 63). The trapezoid is formed by nine city blocks parallel to the river and three in depth. Each city block is also slightly trapezoidal. The square, as in other gridiron examples in urban history, is the result of a decision not to build on the central city block.

Machu Pichu has been the subject of many a book. It is without doubt the most visited and one of the best known of all the Inca ruins. But from the urbanistic point of view it may be considered as atypical. Its location was completely peripheral with respect to the great lines of Inca movement and the areas that were of interest to the Inca rulers, and its position at the summit of a high, narrow promontory 400 meters above the bed of the Urubamba River did not lend itself to the simple urbanistic criteria utilized by the Incas (Fig. 64).

Machu Pichu was never of large size (Fig. 65). Of the two hundred rooms found there, not all could have been used as dwellings. The population would therefore not have exceeded a thousand inhabitants.

Machu Pichu had no over-all layout. The southern sector, which had the best constructed houses, is formed by a series of dwellings along parallel alleyways located on terraces at different levels (Fig. 66). The northern sector is formed, in part, by a series of identical units made up of several dwellings around a courtyard, accessible from a common entrance. The western sector is entirely dedicated to religious constructions. To west and southwest there are two other residential sectors which do not present such a homogeneous pattern as the aforementioned. The whole city is constructed at different levels, and for this reason the topography served not only as a possible hierarchical element for ranking some wards above others, but also as a means of obtaining an extraordinary variety of views. In Machu Pichu there is no street whose length exceeds 100 meters, while frequent stairways offer prospects of the magnificent surroundings which are breathtaking.

It is not quite clear what the functions of Machu Pichu were. The site has natural defenses but the defense constructions are not imposing. It is difficult to understand what effect such a small garrison could have had on invaders coming through the Urubamba valley.[41] It is more logical to suppose that Machu Pichu was an agricultural center. Some small farming settlements have been located right on the slopes of the Urubamba and its vicinity.[42] The extensive terracing done in the vicinity of these settlements and of Machu Pichu itself may have been related to this.

CONCLUSIONS

Pre-Columbian urbanism was not ruled by any single tendency. In Middle America there coexisted contemporaneously an orderly arrangement of high concentration, on the one hand, with rows of houses aligned along visually urban streets (as in Teotihuacán and, centuries later, in Tenochtitlán) and on the other hand, the

Maya concept of low concentration, disorderly organic growth in keeping with natural factors, and the absence of any general plan. Even in South America, where the differences in urban concepts seem to have been regionally less distinct, there are evident disparities between the criteria employed on the north and central coasts and those in the central and southern highlands during a period of growing urbanization and population density such as occurred under the Incas.

The evolution of the pre-Columbian cultures was interrupted at the beginning of the 16th century by the Spanish conquest and colonization. Rather than a superimposition of one culture upon another, there was a partial fusion in which both lost certain of their innate and essential aspects, giving birth to a combination which rarely exhibited the vitality and authenticity of the separate components. Two worlds coexisted during the colonial period: the Spanish, represented in the cities, where the institutions and a way of life imported from the Iberian Peninsula reached their maximum development, and the native, secluded in the rural villages and farmlands, where its values endured almost unchanged, readapting such institutions as were imposed upon it to its own pattern of life.

To a certain extent, native urbanism was prolonged in Spanish America in the form of colonial urbanism. Its influence might pass unnoticed if we do not carefully examine the reasons underlying the selection of location for the first colonial cities by the early Spanish conquerors and governors. Although by the 16th century many of the pre-Columbian cities I have analyzed here had been abandoned for hundreds of years, and apart from rare exceptions the basic criteria for urban layout and design in the pre-Columbian cultures had not been adopted by the Spaniards, it is nevertheless evident that the principal native cities—and even some villages—were utilized by the Spaniards to establish their first regional colonial cities. In other words, the influence of native urbanism on colonial urbanism can be seen in the location of the first colonial cities of the continent and in their plan. Even to this day, more than five centuries after they were conquered, in Mexico City, in Cuzco, and in numerous villages of native origin, land usage and even layouts can be found which functionally constitute modern versions of pre-Columbian usages and which persisted through the colonial period.

NOTES ON THE ILLUSTRATIONS

Numbers refer to figure numbers.

5. Among the classic cities of Middle America, Teotihuacán was possibly the one with the greatest population and area. Recent studies have determined that it covered more than 20 square kilometers, or 2,000 hectares, and that its peak population was at least 50,000 and probably nearer to 100,000. Its population density would then have fluctuated between 25 and 50 people per hectare. There is partial evidence that not all the supposedly urban areas were equally densely populated, nor that the entire area of the city was totally occupied.

8. During its peak period it was customary in Teotihuacán to build a type of dwelling with numerous rooms, which has been called a "palace" or apartment house. Several recently excavated "palaces" show surprising similarities. It was customary to surround each "palace" with an outside wall, not very high and perforated by very few entrances. The over-all ground plan was almost square, based on a module of 57 by 57 meters (or a multiple of it), which seems to have been the standard measurement utilized in the layout of the city's central districts.

10. The population may have been something less than 11,000 within the mapped area, but the full limits of Tikal are still, as with any Maya center, very difficult to define, if they existed at all. The density of the nine central square kilometers (with the principal temples at the center) has been estimated at 8.99 inhabitants per hectare, but it drops to 6.75 if the area is extended to the sixteen square kilometers of the map area.

11. Whether the "palaces" were residences is still not clear. But if this had been so, then the Central Acropolis of Tikal, which covers approximately three hectares, would have been one of the noteworthy pre-Columbian residential groups, despite limited constructional techniques. Among the Mayas of the Petén, ignorance of the pointed arch imposed spatial limitations which led to the construction of long, narrow rooms, badly lit and difficult to organize internally to fulfill functions other than those of a simple refuge.

19. Mayapán was an important center in the peninsula of Yucatán during the centuries which followed the decline of Chichén-Itzá. For reasons which have not been clearly established, an area of 420 hectares was surrounded by an oval-shaped wall of up to two meters in height. Some 2,500 individual ruins have been mapped but it is almost certain that the number of family groups was much less than that of the mapped structures. Dividing the number of individual ruins by two or three we obtain 1,750 or 1,166 family groups, or a total population of between 8,750 and 5,830 people. The total density would have varied between 20.8 and 13.8 persons per hectare. Concentration of individual ruins is higher around the *cenotes*.

32. By uniting the islands of Tenochtitlán and Tlatelolco and providing for their continuous expansion through the addition of new floating islands or *chinampas*, the total area of the Aztec capital may have reached some 750 hectares around the year 1520, of which only 190 would have been on solid ground.

33. Although the plan contains gross mistakes, most of the important urban elements of the Aztec capital are represented. Several ancient and modern authors have estimated the population of Tenochtitlán at an improbable 300,000 inhabitants living in 60,000 houses. Even more difficult to believe is the "120,000 houses" estimated by Torquemada or the "80,000 to 100,000 homes of seven persons" allowed by Soustelle. These figures are simply impossible for an area of 750 hectares approximately 75% of which were floating *chinampas*. To judge by the densities possible in districts of solid ground and in districts of *chinampas*, I suggest a total population of some 65,000 inhabitants.

36. The architecture of the Aztec palaces was sober and without exterior ornamentation. The palaces were exceedingly spacious and organized around courtyards. The palace of Montezuma II was his place of residence and at the same time served as the center of government of the Aztec state and as lodging for numerous guests.

45. Estimates of the total population of Chan Chan are unreliable. There is no doubt that we are dealing with a very extensive city, possibly the most highly populated of any pre-Columbian city of Peru, in which areas of high density, such as the citadels, alternated with others that were less concentrated.

53. The layout of the colonial city respected the essential lines of the Inca city. According to those who knew it when it was still the capital of the Inca rulers, it would have had some 4,000 dwellings, although many times this number of houses must have been scattered through the suburbs. One witness of the conquest, Pedro Sancho, assigned to the valley in which the city is constructed a population occupying more than 100,000 houses. This combined with similar testimony from others in the conquest gives us the picture of a very confined, highly concentrated and densely populated center surrounded by a series of modest suburbs interspersed with cultivated land.

55. In the center of Cuzco, after the remodeling ordered by Pachacuti, every Inca constructed his own palace, so that on the arrival of the Spaniards they surrounded the Aucaipata, the present-day Plaza de Armas (1). The palace of Viracocha Inca (a) was located approximately where the Cathedral now stands (E). To the south were the palaces of Pachacuti (b) and Huascar (e). Also surrounding the square or close to it were the school for the nobles (c), the house of the Virgins of the Sun (f), and the palace of Tupac Yupanqui (g). The palaces of the Inca chiefs were fairly large. Externally they had long solid walls of fine-hewn stone, broken here and there by a door. Internally, the rooms were arranged according to function around courtyards although, due to the cold but sunny climate of the highlands, there were hardly any windows.

56. It is still possible to admire the skill of Inca stonemasons in the walls of the extant palaces and temples which the stroller encounters as the facade of a street, the base of a church, or the framework of a colonial gateway. It would seem that different qualities of stone were used according to the importance of the buildings. Thus, a hard, dark, nearly black stone was used in the constructions of the center, while the more common types, such as diorite and limestone, were used for fortifications and other general purposes. Nevertheless, it was "adobe" or clay, in the form of large blocks, which was the most frequently used construction material.

61. In no pre-Columbian state were projects of regional infrastructure so essential to its proper functioning as under Inca rule. If it is accepted that regional interrelationships can be taken as a measure of the level of political and economic integration reached by the various territorial areas of a state, it is evident that the Inca empire was the culmination of successive and progressive experiments in pre-Columbian South America. Nothing like it existed in Middle America. The area covered by the Inca regional infrastructure constitutes a measure of the area which they were able to control effectively. The roads, suitable for each type of topography, the bridges, and the storerooms for supplies were essential for the maintenance of communications. In this sense the Inca Empire is the best example of political cohesion and of the utilization of infrastructural programs to that end. Their roads and aqueducts also demonstrate the measure of expansion attained by the pre-Inca states, such as the Mochica and Chimú on the northern coast and the Nazca on the central coast.

NOTES

1. "The world of Teotihuacán, guided by gods and priests, is a theocracy that reaches an epoch of unprecedented splendor." (Bernal, 1959). Referring to the classic centuries, Wolf says: "The leading figure of the society dominated by the ceremonial center is the full-time servant of the gods on whose mediation between supernatural and human beings the welfare of man depends." (Wolf, 1959.) It is generally accepted that theocratic government existed in the central plateau of Mexico at least since the middle formative period. But it has been suggested that the government of the Olmecs was not a theocracy and that during the flourishing of the Olmec centers along the coast of the Gulf of Mexico priests played a secondary role. Certain families may have inherited control of certain sites, and they may have organized actual states.

2. This is the classification employed by Angel Palerm and Eric Wolf in their essay "Estudios sobre ecología humana," *Estudios y monografías*, III, Union panamericana, Washington, D.C., 1960.

3. A temple with stone walls, probably dating from before 2000 B.C., was discovered at Kotosh. near Huanuco, in the central highlands of Peru by a scientific expedition from the University of Tokyo. S. Izumi and T. Sono, *Andes 2: Excavations at Kotosh, Peru*, Tokyo, 1963.

4. Two well-known scholars jointly express their point of view in relation to these migrations: "Any theory of population spread into these areas [Middle and South America] must assume north to south movements of peoples and cultures in a lithic stage of development." (Willey and Phillips, 1958.)

5. For a brief up-to-date summary of the Olmec culture: M. D. Coe, D. A. Diehl, and M. Stuwer, "Olmec Civilization, Veracruz, Mexico: Dating of the San Lorenzo Phase," *Science*, Vol. 155, No. 3768, March 1967, pp. 1399–1401.

6. P. H. Drucker, R. F. Heizer, and R. J. Squier, "Excavations at La Venta, Tabasco," Smithsonian Institution, Washington, D.C., 1955.

7. Personal communication from Dr. Michael Coe.

8. The base of the Pyramid of the Sun is about 230 meters square. The Pyramid's height is close to 70 meters.

9. The Pyramid of the Sun was reconstructed by Leopoldo Batres in the early years of this century. It was originally formed of four horizontal units.

10. No roads have been discovered in the Petén. Even two such important neighboring centers as Tikal and Uaxactún were not connected by any roads during the classic period. In Yucatán remains of paved roads have been discovered, but they do not appear to have formed part of a network. The most important causeway known in Yucatán connected Yaxuná with Cobá over a distance of 99 kilometers.

11. "The size of the individual milpa is the determining factor for returning daily instead of by the week.... Those milpas visited daily are generally the smallest, that is from $1\frac{1}{2}$ to 3 acres in size, instead of 4 acres or more." R. Reina, "Milpas and Milperos: Implications for Prehistoric Times," *American Anthropologist*, Vol. 69, 1967, pp. 1–20.

12. Unless it was for religious reasons, it is difficult to explain an average width of 75 meters for the Mendez causeway, which was the broadest, connecting the Temple of the Inscriptions with the central complex, and an average width of over 35 meters for the Maler causeway, the narrowest, linking the north group with the central complex. All the causeways found at Tikal were paved, edged by low masonry walls, and constructed during the late classic period, but it is possible that they existed centuries earlier in rougher form.

13. The pre-classic period at Tikal extended from 600 B.C. to 250 A.D. "It was a time of experimentation with a none too easy environment, of adaptation both to the environment and very likely to the brilliant trends of their Meso-American neighbors." (W. Coe, 1965.)

14. Temple I stands almost 50 meters high. It had nine terraces.

15. A section of the North Acropolis representing "about 1,000 years of construction" is shown on pages 28 and 29 of the special issue of *Expedition* on Tikal (W. Coe, 1965).

16. It is not possible to establish exactly how the form of the central complex of Tikal evolved, nor to determine whether a changing conception of urban spaces came about with the passage of time, as was the case with architectural style.

17. The north group of Chichén-Itzá is perhaps the best example of Toltec influence on the architecture and urban design of the Yucatán Mayas.

18. A recent map of Dzibilchaltún also shows a vast, sparsely settled area. Several causeways connected the principal groups of buildings. As in Tikal, the higher densities of occupation are near the main center. However, what appears to have been the main axis of movement at Dzibilchaltún connects a row of three centers with a straight causeway of more than 2,000 meters in length.

19. Ce Acatl Copiltzin was born near Tepoztlan, where the cult of Quetzalcoatl was practiced, and lived in exile for many years until he took power with the help of his father's partisans. He adopted the name of Quetzalcoatl after he became a priest of the cult of that god.

20. One of the best general descriptions of the physical characteristics of the indigenous cities in the decades following the conquest can be read in Motolinia (1941). His real name was Fray [Friar] Toribio de Benavente.

21. The pyramid of the twin temples dedicated to the cults of Huitzilópochtli and Tlaloc was consecrated in 1487, during the reign of Ahuizotl. Tlaloc, the rain god, was one of the oldest of Mexico; he was known as Chac among the Maya and Cocijo among the Zapotecs. Huitzilópochtli, the war god, was the most worshiped god among the Aztecs.

22. The principal axis of the great Temple of Tenochtitlán was east-west. Perfect bilateral symmetry was not achieved in the physical layout of the Great Temple, although the different buildings were situated with obvious attention to formal balance.

23. Personal communication from Prof. Carlos Ponce Sanginés.

24. A. Kidder II, L. G. Lumbreras and D. S. Smith, "Cultural development in the Central Andes—Peru and Bolivia" (Meggers and Evans, 1963, pp. 89–101).

25. D. Collier, "The Central Andes" (Braidwood and Willey, 1962, pp. 165–176).

26. The Gallinazo group was one of the most extensive classic settlements in the Virú valley, although it only occupied an area of eight hectares around a central pyramidal mound. For a detailed study of the Gallinazo group see W. C. Bennett, *The Gallinazo Group*, Yale University Press, New Haven, 1950.

27. D. E. Thompson, "Post-Classic Innovations in Architecture and Settlement Patterns in the Casma Valley, Peru," *Southwestern Journal of Anthropology*, Vol. 20, No. 1, 1964, pp. 91–105.

28. *Op. cit.*, p. 93.

29. In the Casma valley, molded mud-brick and thick clay walls of trapezoidal sections were used for the first time. In the Virú valley a road some 10 meters wide was built across the valley from southeast to northwest.

30. It has been estimated that the first ruler of the Chimú kingdom took power in the first half of the 14th century and that the capital of the kingdom was cap-

tured between 1463 and 1471, when the armies of Pachacuti and Topa Inca conquered the northern and central coast and the northern highlands all the way up to Quito and Manta.

31. For a detailed analysis of the *huaca* El Dragón located not far from the northern peripheral wall of Chan Chan: R. P. Schaedel, "The Huaca El Dragón," *Journal de la Société des Américanistes de Paris*, Tome LV-2, 1966, pp. 383–496. Schaedel says: "There is little reason to doubt that the huaca was a temple, i.e., a structure dedicated to cult activities," p. 450.

32. E. George Squier, Peru, *Incidents of Travel and Exploration in the Land of the Incas*, Hurst & Co., New York, 1877.

33. H. Horkheimer, *Historia del Perú; Perú prehispanico*, Trujillo, 1943.

34. W. C. Bennett, "The Archaeology of the Central Andes," J. H. Steward, editor, in *The Andrean Civilizations* (1946), and J. Alden Mason, *The Ancient Civilizations of Perú* (1957).

35. Luís Miró Quesada, "Chan Chan, estudio de habilitación urbanística," manuscrito inédito, O.N.P.U., Lima, 1957.

36. Some years ago architect Emilio Harth Terre expressed this point of view in a personal communication.

37. "The empire of the Incas combined the most absolute despotism with social and political indulgence toward the peoples subdued." (Metraux, 1962.)

38. John H. Rowe, "Urban Settlements in Ancient Peru," *Nawpa Pacha*, No. 1, Berkeley, 1963.

39. Hernando Pizarro, "Carta a los oidores de la audiencia de Santo Domingo," in *Tres testigos de la conquista del Perú*, Colección Austral, No. 1168, Buenos Aires, 1953.

40. D. Shea, "El conjunto arquitectónico central en la Plaza de Huanuco Viejo," *Cuadernos de Investigación*, Universidad Nacional Hermilio Valdizan, No. 1, Huanuco, 1966.

41. Eighty percent of the bodies found at Machu Pichu were of women. However, considering that the city remained inhabited for decades after the conquest, some change in the composition of the population could have taken place.

42. For a description of these settlements: P. Fejos, *Archaeological Explorations in the Cordillera Vilcabamba, Southeastern Peru*, Viking Fund, New York, 1944.

BIBLIOGRAPHY

Five years ago I wrote a brief introduction to a more extensive bibliography on the subject of pre-Columbian cities (Hardoy, 1964). Since then several publications fundamentally related to the subject of this volume have been published, preliminary reports of research under way have been circulated, and many articles, essays, and summaries have appeared in scientific periodicals all attesting to the growing interest of scholars in the study of pre-Columbian cultures.

The basic bibliography presented here cannot do justice to the numerous authors who have contributed through the years to the knowledge of pre-Columbian cultures. In preparing it I have followed three criteria of selection: a) those works most representative of the groups into which the bibliography is divided, b) priority to books and essays, rather than articles and reports, c) English editions, where I am aware of their existence, otherwise Spanish or French editions.

GENERAL SOURCES

Cieza de Leon, Pedro de, *La crónica del Perú*, Espasa Calpe Argentina, Buenos Aires, 1945. English edition: ———, *The Travels of Pedro de Cieza de Léon from 1532 to 1550*, 2 vol. translated and edited by Clements R. Markham, Burt Franklin, 1964.

Cobo, Bernabé, *Historia del Nuevo Mundo*, Cuzco, 1956.

Cortés, Hernán, *Cartas de relación de la conquista de Mexico*, Espasa Calpe Argentina, Buenos Aires, 1961.

Diaz del Castillo, Bernal, *Historia verdadera de la conquista de la Nueva España*, Espasa Calpe Argentina, Buenos Aires, 1955. English edition: ———, *The Discovery and Conquest of Mexico 1517–1521*, ed. Genaro Garcia, transl. A. P. Maudslay. Introduction to American ed. by Irving A. Leonard, Farrar, Straus & Cudahy, 1956.

Garcilaso de la Vega (El Inca), *Comentarios reales*, Emecé editors, S.A. Buenos Aires, 1943. English edition: ———, *Royal Commentaries of the Incas, and General History of Peru*, translated with an Introduction by Harold V. Livermore, foreword by Arnold J. Toynbee, University of Texas Press, Austin, 1966.

Motolinia, *Historia de los Indios de la Nueva España*, Editorial Salvador Chavez Hayhoe, Mexico, 1941.

Poma de Ayala, Felipe Guaman, *Nueva crónica y buen gobierno*, Institut d'Ethnologie, Paris, 1936.

Sahagún, Fray Bernardino de, *Historia General de las cosas de Nueva España*, Mexico, 1938.

Sancho, Pedro, *Relación de la conquista del Perú*, Ediciones Jose Porrua Turanzas, Mexico, 1962.

MIDDLE AMERICA

Adams, Robert McC., *The Evolution of Urban Society, Early Mesopotamia and Pre-Hispanic Mexico*, Aldine Publishing, Chicago, 1966.

Bernal, Ignacio, *Tenochtitlán en una isla*, Instituto Nacional de Antropología e Historia, Mexico, 1959.

Caso, Alfonso, *The Aztecs, People of the Sun*, University of Oklahoma Press, Norman, 1957.

Coe, Michael, *Mexico*, Frederick A. Praeger, New York, 1966.

————, *The Maya*, Frederick A. Praeger, New York, 1967.

Coe, William, "Tikal: Ten Years of Study of a Maya Ruin in the Lowlands of Guatemala," *Expedition*, Vol. 8, No. 1, Philadelphia, 1965.

Gibson, Charles, *The Aztecs under Spanish Rule*, Stanford University Press, Stanford, 1964.

Krickeberg, Walter, *Las antiguas civilizaciones mexicanas*, Fondo de Cultura Económica, Mexico, 1961.

Morley, Sylvanus, *The Ancient Maya*, revised by G. W. Brainerd, Stanford University Press, Stanford, 1956.

Palerm, A. and Wolf, E., "La agricultura y el desarrollo de la civilización en Mesoamérica," *Revista Interamericana de Ciencias Sociales*, Vol. 1, No. 1, Washington, D.C., 1961.

Peterson, Frederick, *Ancient Mexico*, G. P. Putnam's Sons, New York, 1959.

Sanders, William T., *The Cultural Ecology of the Teotihuacán Valley*, Pennsylvania State University Press, University Park, 1965. A preliminary report.

Soustelle, Jacques, *La vida cotidiana de los aztecas*, Fondo de Cultura Económica, Mexico, 1956.

Thompson, J. Eric, *The Rise and Fall of Maya Civilization*, University of Oklahoma Press, Norman, 1954.

Vaillant, George, *The Aztecs of Mexico*, revised by Suzannah B. Vaillant, Doubleday and Company, New York, 1962.

Vogt, E. Z. and Ruz, A. (eds.), *Desarrollo cultural de los mayas*, Mexico, 1964.

Wauchope, Robert (ed.), *Handbook of Middle American Indians*, Vols. 1–5 published, University of Texas Press, Austin, 1964.

Wolf, Eric, *Sons of the Shaking Earth*, University of Chicago Press, Chicago, 1959.

SOUTH AMERICA

Bennett, W. C. and Bird, J. C., *Andean Culture History*, second revised edition, Natural History Press, New York, 1964.

Bingham, Hiram, *Machu Pichu, A Citadel of the Incas*, Yale University Press, New Haven, 1930.

Brundage, B. C., *Empire of the Inca*, University of Oklahoma Press, Norman, 1963.

Bushnell, G. H. S., *Perú*, Frederick A. Praeger, New York, 1963.

Kosok, Paul, *Life, Land and Water in Ancient Perú*, Long Island University Press, New York, 1965.

Mason, J. Alden, *The Ancient Civilizations of Perú*, Pelican Books, Harmondsworth, 1957.

Metraux, Alfred, *Les Incas*, Editions du Seuil, Paris, 1963.

Moore, Sally F., *Power and Property in Inca Perú*, Columbia University Press, New York, 1958.

Steward, Julian (ed.), "The Andean Civilizations," *Handbook of South American Indians*, Vol. 2, U. S. Government Printing Office, Washington, D.C., 1959.

Willey, G. R., *Prehistoric Settlements Patterns in the Virú Valley*, Smithsonian Institution, Washington, D.C., 1953.

ART, ARCHITECTURE AND TOWN PLANNING

Covarrubias, Miguel, *Indian Art of Mexico and Central America*, Alfred A. Knopf, New York, 1957.

Hardoy, Jorge E., *Ciudades Precolombinas*, Ediciones Infinito, Buenos Aires, 1964.

————, and Schaedel, R. P. (eds.), *El proceso de urbanización en América desde sus orígenes hasta el presente*, Centro de Estudios Urbanos y Regionales, Buenos Aires, 1968.

Kelemen, Pál, *Medieval American Art*, The Macmillan Company, New York, 1956.

Kubler, George, *The Art and Architecture of Ancient America*, Penguin Books, Baltimore, 1961.

Marquina, Ignacio, *Arquitectura prehispánica*, Instituto Nacional de Antropología e Historia, Mexico, 1951.

Millon, René, "Teotihuacán," *Scientific American*, Vol. 216, No. 6, New York, 1967.

Proskouriakoff, Tatiana, *An Album of Maya Architecture*, Carnegie Institution, Washington, D. C., 1946.

Séjourné, Laurette, *Arquitectura y pintura en Teotihuacán*, Siglo Veintiuno Editores, Mexico, 1966.

MISCELLANEOUS

Braidwood, R. J. and Willey, G. R. (eds.), *Courses Toward Urban Life*, Aldine Publishing, Chicago, 1962.

Meggers, B. and Evans, C. (eds.), *Aboriginal Cultural Developments in Latin America; An Interpretative Review*, Smithsonian Institution, Washington, D. C., 1963.

Tax, Sol (ed.), *The Civilizations of Ancient America*, University of Chicago Press, Chicago, 1951.

Toussaint, M., Gómez de Orozco, F. and Fernandez, J., *Planos de la ciudad de Mexico*, Siglos XVI y XVII, Mexico, 1938.

Willey, G. R. (ed.), Prehistoric Settlement Patterns in the New World, Johnson Reprint, New York, 1956.

Willey, G. R. and Phillips, P. H., *Method and Theory in American Archaeology*, University of Chicago Press, Chicago, 1958.

INDEX

SOURCES OF ILLUSTRATIONS

Numbers refer to figure numbers.

Aerial Explorations, Inc., (American Geographical Society): 41, 49.

Albert Guillot, Paris (P. Rivet, *Cités Maya*): 15.

American Geographical Society: 47

Carnegie Institute of Washington (Morris R. Jones, *Map of the ruins of Mayapán, Yucatán, Mexico*): 19; (S. Morley, *The Inscriptions of Péten*): 16, 17; (T. Proskouriakoff, *An Album of Maya Architecture*): 18; (O. G. and E. B. Ricketson, *Uaxactún, Guatemala, Group E, 1926, 31*): 20.

Colección Emilio Harth Terré, Lima: 55, 58, 59.

Compañia Mexicana Aerofoto S. A.: 6, 9, 23, 26, 29.

Doubleday and Co., Inc., New York (G. C. Vaillant, *The Aztecs of Mexico*): 31.

Editorial Nueva España, Mexico (B. de Sahagum, *Historia General de las Cosas de Nueva España*): 37

The Geographical Journal, Royal Geographical Society, London: 34.

Guía del Cuzco: 62.

Hardoy, original photographs for plates were supplied by the author: 1–3, 7, 14, 24, 28, 30, 38, 39, 44, 50, 51, 56, 61.

Harper and Brothers, New York (E. G. Squier, *Peru, Incidents of Travel and Exploration in the Lands of the Incas*): 53.

Instituto Nacional de Antropología e Historia de Mexico: 25, 27, 33, 35, 36

Paul Kosok, (American Geographical Society): 40, 43

Library of Congress, Washington D.C.: 32, 54

Lima (Armillas, "Teotihuacán, Tula y los toltecas," *Runa* III, Buenos Aires): 8

© National Geographic Society, Washington, D.C., USA: 66

Oficina Nacional de Planificación y Urbanísmo, Peru: 46, 48

Copyright © 1967 by Scientific American, Inc. All rights reserved. From René Millon, "Teotihuacán," June 1967: 5

Servicio Aerofotográfico Nacional, República del Peru: 45, 52, 57, 63–65

Smithsonian Institution, Washington, D.C.(P. H. Drucker and others, *Excavations at La Venta, Tabasco*): 4

C. W. Sutton (American Geographical Society): 42

University of California Press, Berkeley (T. McCown, *Pre incaic Huamachuco*): 60

The University Museum, University of Pennsylvania, Philadelphia: 12, 13, 21; (R. F. Carr and J. E. Hazard, *The Plan of Tikal*): 10, 11

DATE DUE

Demco, Inc. 38-293